BOOK TESTIMONIALS
Do You Really Want To Be An Entrepreneur?

"This book stands out because of its 'stripped-bare' authenticity. Never once does the reader feel 'less than' because Karel writes from a position of sincere authenticity and unrestrained transparency. The lessons are simple yet vital. The guidance is unembellished and hits to the core of starting, running and growing your business. Well done Karel. It is a truly great read"

Steve Hughes, business owner, radio presenter, business & finance guru

"Every word is truthful and inspirational. I read your book constantly and in five weeks it has helped me to find myself again. It has been one of the hardest and toughest journeys of my life. Thank you, Karel Vermeulen. I highly recommend your book".

Toni Michell, Guest House Entrepreneur, South Africa.

"What I loved about this book is the personal touch. Business is about real people and Karel delivers this so that it reads like a fast-paced novel. If you're looking for a business book that gets past the waffle, this book is for you"

Andre Du Toit, the Big Positive Guy, Professional Speaker and radio presenter.

"I was honoured to receive five personalised copies of your great book, which were distributed to the management team in my company. It is a very practical book that has been set out in such a way that it offers a checklist way of applying your methods, which is positiv business owner. It is a truly magnificent, hands-on book for new business owners, entrepreneurs at any level and management staff looking to improve their divisions within a company. Thank you, Karel, for giving back so generously!"

Roy Westfehling. CEO WESTECH, South Africa's Leading Information Technology Services Company since 1996.

"Such an honour and privilege to meet and befriend such an extraordinary human being, Karel Vermeulen, who constantly pushes boundaries and inspires you to do more. Even more special was that I was able to receive the first-ever signed copy of his book, I didn't mean to start reading the book straight away, but his writing style is so gripping that it makes you want to read more. This book is simply written in such an authentic manner that it speaks directly to you. It is a book that is so interactive and real, that the knowledge jumps out at you and compels you to want to be better and take your life to the next level. It even gives you the tools to do that."

Sameer Charles, Entrepreneur, www.humancapacitybuilding.co.za

"What strikes me the most is that, not only does he share his personal story, but he holds you accountable through various practical exercises at the end of each chapter. I would recommend this book, not only to entrepreneurs, but also to young people who are going into business, to guide them in the direction that they should be going in. From the color of your branding and the personal impact that you, yourself has on your brand, it does not matter what you sell, it is always going to be part of your brand and how to translate your personality into your brand. Follow Karel Vermeulen's steps and create success in your own business and life."

Sari Cohen, Entrepreneur, www.allsuresensuality.co.za

"I am very grateful and blessed that I followed my gut-feeling and listened to that little voice that said, "I need to chat to this guy, because I can learn a lot from him." One of the most epic and life transforming journeys is behind me because of Karel Vermeulen, and a lot of the sound advice and business tips that I have learned are contained within this book. I will forever be indebted to him and highly recommend everyone to read this book."

Andrew Patterson, Entrepreneur,
Motivational Speaker, Philanthropist,
www.365climbs.co.za

"It was amazing to have coaching with Karel and then to get his book. I only got halfway through the book because my teenage son, who is 16 years old, wanted to read it first. I was shocked when Karel, my coach, said that he wanted to attend my money course. It has been such an incredible journey, and without him I don't think that I would have been able to do what I am doing."

Lisa Rouhana, Money Coach, Love Yourself
Wealthy, www.lisaloveslife.co.za

"Truly an inspirational book that encourages you to face all your difficult challenges, accept them, and move forward. Arming you with the right success tools, the wisdom herein helped me to make sense of my crazy life. Like no other book that I have read, it also serves as an educational manual with exercises at the end of each chapter guiding and assisting you to conquer your own challenges as they arise. Being confronted with the original guidelines of good business, page after page, one is forced to re-evaluate and take stock of your own critical business processes. After reading this book you feel inclined to start all over again. A great piece of literature and essential to every management position."

Chris de Villiers, Entrepreneur and
Business Owner at Continuum Coffee Lab.

"I recently had the privilege of interviewing Karel Vermeulen about his book: 'Do you Really want to be an entrepreneur?' Many business and personal growth nuggets in one book. Love his personal development story in his book. The nugget I took for myself in the book was the 29-second Introduction, which I started implementing immediately. It is a good read"

Jasper Basson, Founder Dryk Holdings, Financial Director: Lead Optimizers, Habit Practitioners, You Tube: Jasper Basson.

"Karel Vermeulen is such an amazing human being. He is more than just a friend and a phenomenal business coach. He is an inspiration. He helps you to see what you already know about yourself. Whether you see it as your ego, or, as he calls it: the jackal inside of you. This book is such an amazing, easy read. I was in a dark, lonely, confused place - constantly living out bad habits and beliefs; and let me tell you, this book has changed my life. I am now living my dream every single day."

Irene Bettencourt, Real Estate Specialist, www.propertycoza.co.za

Do You Really Want to be an Entrepreneur?

Do You Really Want to be an ENTREPRENEUR?

HOW I CREATED A SEVEN-FIGURE BUSINESS IN TWENTY-FOUR MONTHS RIGHT FROM MY KITCHEN TABLE.

KAREL VERMEULEN
Foreword by Erna Basson

NEW YORK

LONDON • NASHVILLE • MELBOURNE • VANCOUVER

Do You Really Want to be an ENTREPRENEUR?

How I Created a Seven-figure Business in Twenty-four Months Right from my Kitchen Table

Published in New York, New York, by Morgan James Publishing. Morgan James is a trademark of Morgan James, LLC. www.MorganJamesPublishing.com

This publication is designed to provide accurate and authoritative information regarding the subject matter covered. It is sold with the understanding that the publisher is not engaged in rendering legal, accounting, or other professional services. If legal advice or other expert assistance is required, the services of a competent professional person should be sought.

ISBN 9781642792188 paperback
ISBN 9781642792195 eBook
ISBN 9781642792751 audiobook
Library of Congress Control Number: 2018909040

Cover and Interior Design by:
Chris Treccani
www.3dogcreative.net

Morgan James is a proud partner of Habitat for Humanity Peninsula and Greater Williamsburg. Partners in building since 2006.

Get involved today! Visit
MorganJamesPublishing.com/giving-back

Dedicated to:
My lovely partner, Joachim Leicht
My biggest fan, my dearest mother, Babsie Vermeulen
My late dad, Leon Vermeulen, and to all my brothers
and my beautiful sister, Helga Wessels,
who always believes in me.

As well as:
Every entrepreneur and business owner
who reads this book.
May you find inspiration and the answers to your challenges
so that you will be the highly successful person
you are destined to be!

The time to
3-2-1- ACTION
is NOW!

BULK DISCOUNTS AVAILABLE

For details, visit: www.thekvbrand.com
Or contact special sales:
Phone: +2778-677-6979
Email: info@thekvbrand.com

PREFACE

Why am I sharing my business life story?

I am sharing this book from a personal perspective. It is my own story about where I was, where I currently find myself, and ultimately, my vision for my business and future. The magnitude of challenges, and how I overcame them (thus far), as well as the mistakes I made during my ongoing journey to continuous success, and how I made my first million with hardly any money or financial backing, will, I hope, pave the way for you to achieve your own dreams.

My business is you. I care about your success, and I believe in you. We all need that special person in our lives who tells and shows us that they genuinely care and truly believes in our ability to become successful. I am that person. With each chapter, I'll take you on an inside journey through my life and business. I believe this will help you relate to your current situation while shedding some light on what you want to achieve—in your business or personal life. Each chapter is carefully selected, detailing diverse influences, decisions, and points. I love being different. I have learned in life that the unique quality of "being different" ultimately makes each one of us special, setting us apart from the rest. I had to learn to embrace it, and I challenge you to embrace "being different" as well. This is a hands-on book, with practical exercises, and a story-line that underscores the lessons I'm sharing with you. This way, I can offer the experience it took to make Lubrimaxxx™, my other businesses, and, ultimately, my personal brand, the enormous success they are today. Being different is the new road map to success. That is what you will experience by reading this book.

TABLE OF CONTENTS

FOREWORD BY ERNA BASSON

What an absolute pleasure and honor it is to write an introduction to my friend, turned best friend, turned business partner, Karel Vermeulen. Karel is the dictionary example of someone who stems from humble beginnings, and despite life's obstacles and disadvantages, achieved tremendous success in his life.

I remember the day so vividly when Karel told me his background and where he came from. A story like none other—filled with challenges, human strength, and, ultimately, hope and joy. We were driving on the highway in Johannesburg, and all I could think was how jaw-dropping and inspiring his story was as it brought tears to my eyes.

Karel has made a tremendous success of his life, starting off with less than nothing, and now owning a very successful multimillion-dollar business. How did he achieve this, you are, no doubt, asking? The answer is simple; he never gave up. Karel is one of the hardest-working, loyal, and genuine people I know, and when he told me that he was going to write a book, I was in awe, knowing what a tremendous inspiration he would be to others.

In true Karel Vermeulen style, this book is loaded with knowledge, secrets, and insider's" know-how," which he is sharing with you. This book is ideal for new and upcoming entrepreneurs, as well as for well-established business owners seeking expert help and guidance. This book will give you the knowledge and tools you need to take your business (and ultimately your life) to the next level.

Get ready to have your life transformed!

ACKNOWLEDGMENTS

I am forever grateful, not ashamed, of my past as it shaped me into the person I became—one able to reach out for help, encouragement, and counsel. I am thankful for the opportunity to acknowledge so many who contributed to my life and this work.

To Peter Marx, my first editor, and Bonnie Hearn Hill, my second, for your belief in me, and for recruiting me into the world of authorship, and for your professional guidance, wisdom, encouragement, and editing throughout this project.

To my beloved mom and family members for your unconditional love and support, and for shaping me in the person I am today.

To Nadia Hearn and her wonderful team of GET-PUBLISHED[1], who took me on as a client and assisted me with all my public relations and marketing—not only with this project, but with Lubrimaxxx personal lubricant.

---

1   Nadia Hearn, www.get-published.co.za

To my dad, who passed away in 2015; thank you for your unconditional love, support, and for being my dad, and the wonderful person you were, as well as for accepting me just the way I am.

To John and Lidia from Welbedacht Nature Reserve[2] in Tulbagh for letting me stay at the beautiful Eagle Cottage, where I could write and finish this project.

To all our IMN (Intelligent Millionaire Network)[3] members for your excitement and encouragement with this project. You are a true inspiration to me.

To Cherie Eilertsen, my first one-on-one coach. Thanks for your wisdom, knowledge, love, energy, and encouragement for me to be the best entrepreneur I can, and for transforming my business into a success, as well as for being my friend.

To Erna Basson, my business coach, business partner and friend, who wrote the foreword. What a remarkable, dynamic, and beautiful woman you are! Thank you for your friendship, encouragement, guidance, and coaching, not only on this project, but throughout our new friendship.

To Dan Woodruff, Michael and Robbie Mathews, Michael Jordan, Christine Nielsen, Robin Booth and Erna Basson, who unconditionally and immediately said "yes" when I asked if they would share some of their wisdom,

---

2   Welbedacht Nature Reserve, South Africa, www.welbedachtnaturereserve.co.za

3   Intelligent Millionaires Network, www.intelligentmillionairesnetwork.com

tips, and quotes that helped them become the successful entrepreneurs they are today. I am eternally grateful.

To Joachim Leicht. My lifetime partner, best friend, confidante, and sounding board. Thank you for your sacrifice, understanding, encouragement, patience, love, and support. You are the joy of my life; I love you for who you are, and I love you more than words can express.

My new friend and agent, Jeff Lazarus, from Branded with Authority USA. Without you, this book would still be a manuscript.

Special thank you to Eloise Meyer for taking the time to design the first stunning layout for this book. You knew what I was looking for, and you delivered more than I expected.

To Steve Hughes from Communimail who is one of my business partners, thank you for keeping an eagle eye on the editing.

And last, thank you to David Hancock from Morgan James Publishing for believing in my message, accepting my manuscript and for publishing my book. I am forever grateful to you and your team.

INTRODUCTION

A brief look at entrepreneurial statistics

Although I'm mostly left-brained, I believe I'm a right-brained person: I do not like numbers. However, I had to learn the importance of knowing numbers in business as one of the vital tools needed to succeed. In Chapter Seven, I'll cover "Knowing Your Numbers." Numbers and statistics are crucial to any business, so let us briefly look at the entrepreneurial statistics globally. This is probably more for the left-brainers among us, so for the right-brainers, bear it out—it's of great value.

The global economic landscape has been influenced by a variety of challenges. The Global Entrepreneurship Monitor (GEM)[4] is the world's foremost study on entrepreneurship. Annually, the GEM provides high-quality

---

4   The Global Entrepreneurship Monitor (GEM) www.gemconsortium. org

information, comprehensive reports, and interesting stories, which significantly enhance our understanding of the entrepreneurial phenomenon around the world.

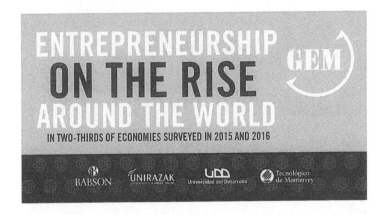

Surprising Findings of This Massive Global Social Entrepreneurship Study[5]

People across cultures, demographics, and continents believe business is about more than making a profit. It's about doing good for others. That's according to a new report released by the Global Entrepreneurship Monitor GEM in assessing social entrepreneurship worldwide. The program, sponsored by Babson College and partnering institutions, provides snapshots of social entrepreneurship by region.

Researchers conducted interviews with 167,793 adults in fifty-eight different economies in 2015. To gauge the prevalence of social entrepreneurship broadly, the researchers

5   Lindsay Friedman (https://www.entrepreneur.com/article/27685)

found a global average rate of 3.2 percent of individuals surveyed were in the start-up phase of social enterprise.

Social entrepreneurs do not only focus on what goes into their pockets, but also on how they can use their platform to give back. In fact, about 52 percent of those included in the survey reinvested profits into social initiatives. In the US, many socially focused companies, such as Yoobi[6] an Tom's of Maine[7], have become household names. But this trend trickles down to smaller economies. The study goes on to explain how the social entrepreneurship trend transcends education levels in many regions.

"Social entrepreneurship is about people starting any initiative that has a social, environmental, or community objective," says Siri Terjesen, a professor at American University who co-authored the report, as stated in a press release.[8] "It could be students who are starting a product that's based on recycled materials, or a group working to find a solution to irrigation problems in their neighbourhood."

Although the popularity of such efforts seems to be far-reaching on the global scale, some countries were more entrepreneurial on the social side than others. For example, of the surveyed population in Senegal, 18.1 percent were pursuing social entrepreneurial activity. In contrast, Taiwan had a rate of only 1.3 percent. The US and Australia were among the nations with the highest levels of activity, each at around 11 percent.

---

6   (https://yoobi.com)
7   (www.toms.com)
8   (http://www.eurekalert.org/pub_releases/2016-06/au-nsro53116.php)

The frequency of commercial start-up pursuits was, of course, found to be a bit higher, with all regions studied averaging at about 7.6 percent. But some nations lead in both categories: Peru has a 10.1 percent rate of individuals working to launch social start-ups, and a 22.2 percent rate of those who are in the process of getting commercial enterprises off the ground.

A gender breakdown also provided interesting insights. Researchers discovered the world's social entrepreneurs are 55 percent male and 45 percent female, a significantly smaller gap compared with commercial counterparts.

"The social entrepreneurship gender gap is less pronounced than in commercial entrepreneurship where men trump women as business leaders 2:1," Terjesen says. "In social ventures, both genders are equally represented, suggesting that social entrepreneurship is a top business field of interest for women worldwide."

While some would figure many social entrepreneurs are of a younger demographic (typically between the ages of eighteen and thirty-four), that's not the case everywhere. In many areas–including Australia and the United States–about 60 percent or more of the proportion of those engaging in social entrepreneurship are older than thirty-five.

How these entrepreneurs get their start seems to be in a similar stride because most use personal funds to get the wheels turning. For instance, the majority (about 60 percent) of those in this part of industry used their own funds to invest in their businesses in Southern and Eastern Asia, the Middle

East, and North Africa. However, sub-Saharan Africa had a low personal investment rate of about 30 percent.

So, what's the reason for the popularity of social entrepreneurship? Terjesen attributes it to the limited ability governments have to solve the increasingly prominent social issues in today's society. Although the growth in the number of socially minded companies is a big step toward achieving those goals, Terjesen says it is important to "determine the most appropriate ways to support social entrepreneurs and scale up their solutions."

Ryan Westwood[9] said that approximately 50 million businesses are launched every year, and experts say three out of four fail. The pressure to achieve success is enormous, and the stress to defy the odds extends beyond the workroom.

"While there are many conversations about the business challenges of a start-up, few voice concerns about the psychological effects of entrepreneurship. What guides the entrepreneurial spirit amid stifling emotional hardship, and how can an entrepreneur survive the process?"

9   Ryan Westwood, Forbes Magazine, January 8, 2016

Why this book? And how it came about

Writing a book was the last thing on my mind because I have never attempted anything like this. Yes, I have written manuscripts for my bachelor's degree in ministry, but most certainly nothing like this. This book is the result of the culmination of my writings and life experience. I realized that I have a great deal to share with my readers—not just my story, but how what I learned can help other people—including you.

The purpose of my book is four-fold. First, as an inspiration and motivation for you to write your own successful story, and I know you can. I am sharing a part of my personal life and entrepreneurial story–my journey of how I started from the bottom with nothing to my name, and how, from my small kitchen flat in Cape Town, I developed and created, in today's terms, a highly successful product brand, Lubrimaxxx™.[10] I did this with neither financial backing nor any knowledge of business or product formulation.

Next, it is an educational and practical book geared toward assisting you in overcoming your fears, doubts, and insecurities, while empowering you to start and grow your own business as you reach your goals and potential.

Furthermore, I'll be sharing what I've learned—what works and what doesn't—so you won't make the same mistakes I've made. As they say: "Only a fool learns from his own mistakes. The wise man learns from the mistakes of

---

10 Lubrimaxxx Personal Lubricant, www.lubrimaxxx.com

others." You must be a very wise person for reading my book right now.

Finally, I want to encourage you. I will be sharing tips and quotes from highly successful international entrepreneurs illustrating what they have learned to make their businesses successful.

My entrepreneurial giant is awake and alive. I want the same for you. Your results are our shared success. My business is you!

Picture Above: The forest cottage where I finished my book manuscript in one week.

Picture to the Left: First drafting of my book. Title was Yes You Can. The title changed as the book evolved.

CHAPTER 1

LUBRIMAXXX™

The Story Behind the Story

On February 26, 2017, at a wealth conference in Johannesburg I was fortunate to be introduced to 1500 attendees from sixty different countries as "The Lube Guy." Since then, everyone knows me by this nickname. Even my friends call me "Mr Lube" or "Karel Condom." Very funny. Or not. You can decide for yourself.

I was not born a natural entrepreneur. I never thought I would be a successful business owner, running five different companies and brands. Circumstances led me to it, but let's start from the beginning.

I am one of five children born to wonderful parents, Leon and Babs Vermeulen. We are four boys and one girl, and we were raised financially challenged in the Free State town of Virginia in South Africa, where my father worked in the gold mines for thirty-two years.

From a very young age, I knew I was different, not like my brothers or the other boys at school. I learned to play classical piano, had no interest in sports, and did not excel in any other school activities. As a result, I was bullied for most of my school days. Even during high school, I was continuously bullied by a few guys just for having a loud voice.

This resulted in my growing up hating myself, hating my voice, and hating my life in general. With low self-esteem, it's no surprise that I became extremely introverted. This later negatively affected my life through various self-destructive patterns, especially jumping from one job to the other. No money was available to go and study further, so I had to find work immediately after I matriculated.

In short, I went from the SA Police Force, to a missionary worker, to a butler. I loved being a butler, especially working in the Middle East for the famous Ritz-Carlton Hotel group as head butler. This was my first experience with top VIPs, celebrities, ambassadors, and ministers. My most cherished photograph is with ex-British Prime Minister, Tony Blair's wife, Cherie Blair, as I held their little son, Leo, on my hip.

I qualified as a massage therapist, personal trainer, and spinning instructor while working in the Middle East and then went on to Antiqua, where I met and massaged the famous actor, John Travolta, twice. What a gentle giant of a gentleman! Later in my journey I had the amazing opportunity to interview him in Los Angeles in front of a crowd of 1,500 people from seventy-one different countries. That moment is forever captured in my memory. I also worked on two cruise ships, a guest house, and I ended up starting my own massage practice in Cape Town. This was my first venture as an entrepreneur.

Oh, do I know what it feels like to be broke, not to have any money. I have been there so many times in my life. I remember the days when I would walk in the street with my eyes focused on the ground to see if someone had mistakenly dropped some money. There was a time in my life when I stole water in the evenings from the neighbors and made a fire on my balcony to boil water for coffee and food because I had no money to pay for electricity and water. One thing I will never forget is when Heidi, a lady from our church, asked me if she could get me anything, and I replied, "If only I can have a bar of soap to wash myself, I would be forever grateful."

So, you see, I know exactly what it is to not have any money at all, what it is to be completely broke. Never in that time, did I ask my parents for money, simply because I had too much pride, and I knew that they were also struggling to make ends meet.

My lightbulb moment

At this time in Cape Town, working as a massage therapist out of my flat, I had my "lightbulb" moment. I stood at my massage-product trolley, and an idea popped into my head. "Why not start making your own skincare products?" Heck yes, it sounded good, but where would I start? I had no formulation background, nor biology or chemical experience of any kind. I left mathematics in grade ten because I disliked the teacher and took up accounting instead of biology and chemistry! What was particularly interesting about this thought, though, was that it did not just sit in my head.

Instead, I felt it slowly make its way toward my heart. This is incredibly important, and it goes beyond just sounding poetic. Your idea needs to be rooted in your heart if you want it to succeed. It needs to consume you entirely.

Well, I had to start somewhere with this skincare idea. I asked many people I knew and some I didn't, but no one seemed to be able to help me. Then I recalled that one of my clients had a successful skincare line and, on their packaging, were the words, "carefully hand blended." Then I thought, *Wow, I can do that*! So, I went to a retail store and bought a box of aqua cream and started mixing it with aromatic oils. (I had some knowledge about that based on my experience as a massage therapist.). Then I learned that the petroleum in the aqua cream is not good for your skin, and that it blocks your pores. I did not like that idea, so I threw it all away.

I will never forget. It was a Tuesday morning about 3 a.m. when I found this guy in Ireland who teaches people to create their own organic skincare products from scratch. Wow, this was my answer! I discovered that he offered a workshop every single weekend, but only in the UK. *Well, there goes that idea*, I thought. However, I bought a sample package and made my first five liters of organic skincare. I was absolutely hooked! I was astonished and couldn't believe it came out perfectly That's how Karl de L'Eau Natural Skincare[11] was born and registered as a company in January 2010. To this day, KDL Skincare is my holding company.

11　Karl de L'Eau Natural Skincare, www.kdlskincare.com

Lubrimaxxx™

"So, how did Lubrimaxxx come about?" That's the question I get asked the most. The same lightbulb scenario as with the skincare range played itself repeatedly in my head: "Why not make my own personal lubricant?" During my market research, I found the following five eye-opening and important factors that pushed me forward in developing my distinct product brand and finding my individual selling proposition (USP). I identified the problem and I created the solution. 1. Most personal lubricants are expensive. 2. Many women experience vaginal dryness due to various contributing factors. 3. A high percentage of men experience some sort of dry spell when it comes to sexual arousal. 4. Most water-based personal lubricants dry out quickly. 5. Most water-based lubricants become sticky. I believe this was mostly because I did not like the lubricants available on the market; most of them were imported, making them ridiculously expensive. From seminars I attended, I learned that if you cannot create a product from scratch, look at what's out there you like, and then figure out how you can improve it and make it more cost-effective. It is important that you need to find your unique selling proposition (USP). That is what I did, and Lubrimaxxx personal lubricant was born. I questioned the available lube products that I did not like (they were expensive, they dried out or got sticky quickly, and they tended to stain linen). I knew I needed to create a lube that eliminated all these negative factors. I searched Google, asked around, and examined different packaging in the shops. That way, I learned about the specific ingredients that go into a water-based lubricant.

I had to look deep in my kitchen cupboards to see what I had that could make these improvements. With much trial and error, I found the right formula. First, I had to test it on myself before I gave it to friends for their honest feedback. Based on what they said, I adjusted the formulations and, after a short while—voila! I found my secret main ingredient that made me a millionaire.

Now, if my kitchen walls could talk and write down what they saw, it would take *Fifty Shades of Grey* to a whole new level.

Product testing

The proof is in the pudding One of the best ways to get product credibility is to test your product or service. However, testing can be very expensive. One inexpensive way to do "clinical testing" for your product is to make samples and give them to your friends, requesting they report back to you. That's exactly what I did. I couldn't think of a better way, considering the fact that I had no money to send my products for expensive testing procedures. As I received feedback, I changed the formula accordingly, and so can you. Just make sure that you keep a logbook for reference. This is one of the best ways to test your product before you go into mass production.

Finding a name and logo

Have you ever seen a company or product name, and your first thought was, *what in the world are they selling*? Exactly! It's important that you choose a product name and logo that says exactly what you are making available to consumers. People shouldn't have to Google your product name, logo, or company to find out what they represent and stand for. Let us take Lubrimaxxx, for example. "Lubri" stands for lubricant, and "maxxx" represents maximum pleasure. The "xxx" at the end of my product name represents that it is a sexual product. My product name is also my logo. You see? No confusion here!

Finding the right name for your product or business can be tricky and an initial headache. If you are clever, you can come up with it yourself, or you can do what I did. I gathered a few of my closest and most trusted friends for a pizza-and-beer evening, and we brainstormed together. Naturally, it must be people that you trust. One guy sat with a laptop and Googled all the names we came up with. I can totally recommend this. What a fun way to search for a name for your product or brand.

Be sure to tell the group exactly what your product or service is all about and what you want to achieve.

Choosing the correct color for your brand

We had fun deciding what colors I should choose for my new brand, Lubrimaxxx. We Googled a lot of lubricant brands, examining their main color schemes, all the while asking ourselves what emotions we felt when looking at certain colors. Oh, my, I don't dare mention the answers that came up with certain brands!

Through this exercise, I realized the importance of the correct color scheme for brand packaging. It is all about the message that you want to convey to your potential customer.

Lubrimaxxx's main colors are red, black, white, and gray. Why these colors? Red with a sexual product represents sensuality, sex appeal, and love. Here, black represents the dark side of the sexual adventurer. White balances the other colors and represents that it is a clean, "tested," reliable product. The gray represents those who do not know what they want sexually but are curious about experimenting.

Understanding color and what it represents in business is essential when you are establishing a business profile.

Color psychology[12] affects our lives in so many ways, yet we often don't realize the impact of these choices on our websites, stationery, packaging, in our retail store or office, for our marketing campaigns, or for our business clothing. Color has a powerful subconscious effect in every aspect of our lives without even saying a word. An understanding of color in business gives us an invaluable tool to get the best response to marketing and promotional efforts and, ultimately, to create a successful business.

In applying the information about color to enhance your own business profile and marketing, do not use any color entirely on its own; it is always best to use a complementary

---

12   http://www.empower-yourself-with-color-psychology.com/color-meanings-in-business.html

color with your main choice because over-use of any one color can negate its effect and, in fact, have the opposite desired effect.

There is almost always more than one option of color combinations to assist your business, so you don't have to choose any color that you don't like, or that doesn't resonate with you. You may even use a color you dislike, in a very small amount, to get the response you want from your clientele. For example, you could use a small amount of red to indicate your passion or energy for your business or as a call-to-action button on your website.

Color Meanings[13][14]

Red is the color of energy, passion, and action

The color red is a warm and positive color associated with our physical needs and our will to survive. It exudes a strong and powerful masculinity and is energizing. Red excites the emotions and motivates us to take action. It signifies a pioneering spirit and leadership qualities, promoting ambition and determination. Red is also strong-willed and can provide confidence to those who are shy or lacking in willpower. Being the color of physical movement, red awakens our physical lifeforce.

It is the color of sexuality and can stimulate deeper and more intimate passions in us, such as love and sex on the

---

13   Color Meanings by Jacob Olesen, www.color-meanings.com
14   Color Meaning and Symbolism: How to use the power of color in your Branding by Rebecca Gross, October 27, 2015

positive side, or revenge and anger on the negative. It is often used to express love, as it does on Valentine's Day. However, it relates more to sexuality and lust, rather than love-love, which is often expressed with pink. At its most positive, it can create life with its sexual energy, or use its negative expression of anger and aggression to fuel war and destruction.

Black is mysterious and protective

Black relates to the hidden, the secretive, and the unknown, and, as a result, it creates an air of mystery. It keeps things bottled up inside, hidden from the world. In color psychology, black gives protection from external emotional stress, and black means power and control, hanging onto information and things rather than giving them out to others. Black implies self-control and discipline, independence, and a strong will, and it gives an impression of authority and power.

Black creates a barrier between itself and the outside world, providing comfort while protecting its emotions and feelings, and hiding its vulnerabilities, insecurities, and lack of self-confidence. Black often is associated with sexiness and seduction, as in the temptress in sexy black lingerie creating an air of mystery and intrigue. It can also imply submission to another (including a sexual partner). So, you can clearly see why the use of black is important to marketing Lubrimaxxx.

Orange is adventurous, self-confident, and risk-taking

In the Western world, orange tends to be the most disliked color. Be careful when using orange in business and apply it sparingly.

In restaurants, cafés, bistros, and diners, it stimulates appetite and conversation, contributing to patrons eating, taking longer and spending more money.

Travel websites should consider it as one of their color choices because of its association with travel, adventure, and exciting, fun times.

Orange is an appealing color for the youth market, and in sports, it encourages energy, flamboyance, and adventure.

Yellow relates to acquired knowledge, lifting and inspiring

Yellow is the color of the mind and intellect. It resonates with the left or logical side of the brain, stimulating our mental faculties, creating mental agility and perception.

Yellow is also uplifting and illuminating, offering hope, happiness, cheerfulness, and fun.

Green is the color of harmony, nature, balance, and growth

Psychologically, it is the color that balances the heart and emotions, creating equilibrium between the head and the heart. It represents growth and is the color of spring, renewal, and rebirth.

It is also the color of nature, which is why many companies using organic or natural ingredients in their products, make use of green on their packaging.

Emotionally, it is a positive color, giving us the ability to love and nurture ourselves and others unconditionally. Green is also associated with health and healing.

Brown it the color of security, protection, and material wealth

Brown is a serious, down-to-earth color, signifying stability, structure, and support.

Relating to the protection and support of the family unit, with a keen sense of duty and responsibility, brown takes its obligations seriously. It encourages a strong need for security and a sense of belonging.

Brown relates to high quality in everything—a comfortable home, the best food, drink, and loyal companionship. It is a color of physical comfort and simplicity. From a negative perspective, it can also give the impression of cheapness and stinginess in certain circumstances.

Brown is friendly and approachable. It is loyal, trustworthy, and dependable in a practical and realistic way.

White is the color of purity, simplicity, innocence, and minimalism

White represents simplicity, purity, innocence and perfection. If you had to identify one brand that has used white to convey its brand message to perfection, it would have to be Apple–white represents the simplicity of the products in both their form and function. In business, it represents cleanliness and hygiene. It indicates calm, simplicity, and organization. On the negative side, some of its meanings include coldness, detachment, sterility, and disinterest. Most businesses use white as backgrounds for their websites. It is ideal for use in infants' products, kitchen and bath appliances, and all other products that wish to portray efficiency and discipline.

White also comes with a starkness or sterility about it, which is often used by designers to convey a minimalistic, aesthetic, and clean, modern quality. It is difficult to inject personality into your brand when using white, so make sure your brand personality is about simplicity, purity, and transparency.

Blue is communicative, trustworthy, and calming, but can also be depressing

Most people love blue because it is also the most universally preferred color. I guess it's because blue is such a versatile color. It's a favorite color for companies wishing to convey reliability, trustworthiness, and communication (I'm looking at you, Facebook, Twitter, and Samsung), and for expressing the authority and officialdom of organizations (oh, hey, there, Constable). Due to its association with sea and sky, blue also is appreciated for its calming and harmonious qualities. However, because of the color's connection with the emotional feeling of being blue, it is also used to express sadness or depression.

Stability and depth are the best expressions of blue as far as its business usage is concerned. Most conservative corporate businesses have blue in some form or another in their logos, business cards, and brochures (marketing material). Similarly, communication, high-tech, computer products, water industry, filtration, swimming-pool cleaning businesses, and similar enterprises always use blue. Health, wellness, and travel industries typically use light blue, while political and religious organizations tend to use dark blue.

Purple is associated with royalty, majesty, spirituality, and the mysterious

Purple is traditionally associated with wealth, wisdom, creativity, royalty, majesty, or nobility, as well as having a spiritual or mysterious quality. Purple is also a low-arousal color.

Darker shades often represent luxury or opulence, while lighter lavender shades are quite feminine, sentimental, and even nostalgic.

It is highly recommended for women and children's products, while many men's products are slowly getting attuned to this color, as well. Use medium purple or violet shades to portray academic brilliance and wisdom. Lavender is considered ideal for home-based businesses selling hand-made products, arts, crafts, and other items of symbolic significance.

I want to congratulate you now that you have read this far. As a business and life transformational coach, I have the wonderful opportunity to meet and work with many amazing people from all walks of life. I have learned that without taking the appropriate action, you will not accomplish and reach your goals.

I want to help you to get started. Will that be okay with you?

At the end of each chapter, you'll find the lessons that I've learned, as well as ten specific exercises that you must complete before you move on to the next chapter in this book. These specific exercises are designed to kick-start your thinking process and help you on your path to success, financial freedom, and to turn your business into one that's profitable.

Remember—I believe in you! You are an entrepreneurial giant!

LESSONS LEARNED

- Be careful when deciding on your color choices for your brand.
- Product testing gives your brand great credibility.
- Your name and logo should state what you do. If your client needs to search for the meaning-you've lost that client.
- Identify a problem and find the solution.
- Do your market research. It's important that you know who your competition is, and what it's doing differently.
- Find your unique selling proposition-USP.
- Your product and or service are simply the vehicles. You need to determine exactly what you are giving your customer. Lubrimaxxx brings back confidence, happiness, and satisfaction in our customers' lives.

Even the smallest or less important thought/idea can become your greatest asset.   Take action!

Exercise 1.

When telling people about your company, do you have to explain what it is you do, or can they see that from your business name?

_____

_____

_____

_____

_____

List all the emotions that you feel when looking at your business colors.

_____

_____

_____

_____

_____

Why did you choose your current business colors?

_____

_____

_____

_____

_____

What are the problems you are solving? Spend some quality time identifying these.

_____

_____

_____

_____

_____

What, aside from your product and/or service, is it that you REALLY provide your customers and/or clients?

_____

_____

_____

_____

_____

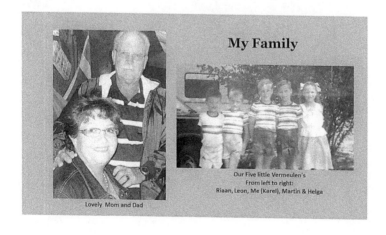

My Family

Our Five little Vermeulen's
From left to right:
Riaan, Leon, Me (Karel), Martin & Helga

Lovely Mom and Dad

South African Police Force

Butler to Cherrie Blair

Strawberry Lube Development

CHAPTER 2

MARKETING AND BRANDING

My First Order

"Right, now, I have a good product, but what now?" I asked myself. I took Lubrimaxxx to Anova Health (my first and current client since December 2011). I handed out little five milliliter lube sachets with the company's safe-sex campaigns on the packaging. They loved it and ordered 30,000 small sachets from me on the spot. Wow was I impressed with myself! After a week, they ordered another 100,000 sachets, and I thought, *Gosh, now I have really made it!*

Never had I had so much money in my bank account, a massive $8600! I felt like the richest man in the world!

"Has your product been tested for osmolality?" the company CEO asked me, as suggested by their Washington head office. What? I didn't even know the word existed. I had to ask around, and back to good old Google I went. To my astonishment, nobody in South Africa could test Lubrimaxxx for osmolality. Although Wits University had an osmometer, no one could operate it. *That's just great,* I thought.

Eventually, I found a company in Boston that builds these osmometers, and they were willing to test my product on ten of their newest machines, free of charge. All it cost me was the DHL delivery cost to send it. The results came through. Lubrimaxxx was very close to human cell osmolality, and Anova Health[15] head office was satisfied. Dr. Kevin Rebe, from Anova Health, then performed a blind test study at the University of Cape Town with some of the most common water-based personal lubricants available in South Africa. These results were published in the *South African Medical Journal* (SAMJ)[16]. Lubrimaxxx was one of the safest of all the products tested!

Then, early one Sunday morning, I got a very disturbing phone call from Alcopac Pharmaceuticals–my packing company. Up to now, I did all the manufacturing myself, on my stove, pouring the product into twenty-five-liter buckets, and then delivering them to the packing company to be packed into the little five-milliliter sachets. They woke me with the disturbing news that, somehow, my product got traces of mold and bacteria in it! I was devastated. How in the world could this happen? I was so careful. I made sure that my whole flat, kitchen, and the equipment were properly sterilized, and I was wearing the correct required protective clothing. We had to throw out the complete batch. I had to make an important decision right then because the order was due for delivery in a few days. Should I give them my formula or not, considering that there was no way I would be able

---

15 Anova Health South Africa, www.anovahealth.co.za
16 South African Medical Journal (SAMJ), January 14, 2014, Vol. 104, no1

to manufacture it all in time? I knew about non-disclosure agreements and decided to outsource all my production and packaging. This was one of the best decisions I made. So, a potentially bad event turned out great.

LESSONS LEARNED

- Put your pride aside and outsource the correct way.
- You cannot do everything yourself

Everything in life happens for a reason. You must take a step back and look for that reason.

The big breakthrough

I applied for a two-year tender contract with Nacosa and Right to Care, two nonprofit and non-government organizations. One criteria were that the lubricant needed to pass a biocompatibility test. Again, I thought, *what in the world is this?* Okay, I won't mention what went through my mind for obvious reasons. Once more, I went through the process of consulting people in the industry: pharmacists, manufacturers, universities, and again, no one could help me. I turned to my new best friend, Google, and found a company in the United States that specialized in biocompatibility testing.[17] This time, I was not as lucky as

---

17   Advanced Instruments, Norwood, USA, 02062

before. I had to pay in advance for these testing procedures, and it would take four months for the results. Damn! I just got my biggest check ever and a nice cash flow. Now, I had to fork out all this money $8,176 for four testing procedures, not knowing if I would pass or not! This test consisted of a Vaginal Test, Cytoxicity Testing, Skin Irritation Testing, and Hypersensitivity Delayed Onset Testing. Big words, I know.

Another requirement of this was that we needed to supply condoms, as well. I manufactured only lubricant. So, what now? I decided to team up with Warren Bell from Quantumed[18], who specialized in condoms, and we formed a successful partnership in the form of a joint venture. He would do the condom side, and I would handle the lube. This was another great lesson I learned, the value of a successful trusted joint venture.

"Shall I do it or not?" A mind battle started. I had to learn to look at the bigger picture, the scope of the two-year possible contract and weigh the pros and cons against each other. This was a huge risk for me. Fortunately, I was brave, and it paid off in the end. I took a deep breath and decided to do it, saying to myself over and over, "What do I have to lose?" I passed all the tests with flying colors and got the contract! During the two years, we distributed more than 19 million five-milliliter lube sachets and condoms all over South Africa, with hardly any delivery mishaps. How amazing is that?

---

18 Quantumed South Africa, www.qzm.co.za

LESSONS LEARNED

- You need to be willing to take calculated risks to succeed. If you do not, you will never know what you are capable of.
- Product testing creates credibility and, therefore, you can charge a higher price.
- When a problem or challenge arises, take time out to step aside and look at the bigger picture. You will be amazed how easy and simple the correct solution is.

The power of a joint venture can be incredibly valuable–even if it is just for a limited period.

In a period of three years, I went from manufacturing in my apartment kitchen, to a small warehouse in Montague Gardens (nearby industrial suburb), and then to a larger warehouse with five offices. This was where I made my first million, and it put me on the map. You see, it takes only one deal or one person to change your life forever.

What is your lightbulb idea? I took that tiny little idea and made it my own. I immediately reacted to it. I made sure that it did not just stay in my head but moved it down to my heart, ensuring that it consumed me, and that I liked the idea. We all get ideas from time to time. What do you do with yours? The faster you react, the faster you will have results.

We live in a society that tends to overthink every little thought. Sometimes, this can be a good thing, but, at other times, not. Overthinking can lead to inaction. I just love this term: "Paralysis by analysis." Do you think about it and then just mark it off as an idea that is too far-fetched, you cannot possibly do it, or do you take that idea and make it part of you?

You must be strategic in your marketing. The only thing that your client or customer is interested in are these words: "What's in it for me?"

You need to be the CEO of your marketing. Who else better to understand your business than yourself? What exactly does this mean? Your job is to come up with the ideas and vision, and then let your team implement them.

Most entrepreneurs believe marketing costs them money, and my response to this is a hefty "BS!" That is old-school thinking. Effective marketing should make you money, not cost you money. You need to get at least three times the return on your marketing investment.

What gets measured gets rewarded. You must have the correct systems in place to measure your marketing strategy.

Every house or building is built on a strong foundation to withstand the forces of nature. Effective marketing also has ten strong fundamentals that you should understand to have successful strategic marketing in place.

STRATEGIC MARKETING FUNDAMENTALS

- Know your numbers. Market by your numbers.
- Ensure your website is at the top 10 percent on Google rankings.
- Understand who your ideal customer is.
- Understand their pains and frustrations.
- How can you solve their true pain?
- Use outstanding tag lines.
- Identify profitable market niches for your business.
- Have a marketing budget and stick to it.
- If possible, invest in a trustworthy public relations company to help you with your marketing and branding messages.
- Be strategic in your business and marketing strategy.

Have a strategic marketing plan of action (it needs to be measurable). To do that, you must have a clear vision and goal of where you want to go and what you want to tell your audience. Next, map it out either on a white board or on paper. On top of that, you need to be specific in all the relevant details. No detail is too small to be left out. Finally, once you have a clear idea of what you're going to do, and how you going to do it, communicate your plan of action to your staff and marketing/sales team, and take immediate action. If you struggle to get this done, ask your business coach.

Finding my USP (Unique Selling Proposition)

USP (Unique Selling Proposition) was another crucial term I had to learn, not just what it meant, but why it mattered. Why did I even need this? Well, I soon found out how important your USP is, and that it will make the difference in closing or not closing a sale.

Wherever I went, my customers all asked the same questions, "What makes your lubricant different from all the other lubricants available?" "Why must we buy your product?" Without hesitation, I proudly proclaimed that our product is the best. Lubrimaxxx is longer-lasting than our competitors, we provide outstanding customer service, and our pricing is, by far, the best! Wrong, wrong, and, again, wrong! These were not the correct answers, I discovered. They are not my USP. They are only some of my benefits and attributes. The result? No sale!

And these are the same type of answers almost everyone in the business proclaims.

I had to set time aside to really dig deep to discover the unique aspects or attributes that make Lubrimaxxx so much better than my competitors' brands. Then, it hit me! When I realized that Lubrimaxxx had passed all these major medical tests, and that the results were published in the *South African Medical Journal*, this was the major difference that set my product apart from my competition. And this also brought me to my big WHY! Lubrimaxxx is all about health and safety, not simply another sexual product. I wasn't just selling your basic lubricant. I was enhancing people's lives, and I had proof that my product was safe.

Branding

Marketing is the engine of your business, while branding is the fuel. Branding gives your brand credibility. Branding makes it so much easier for you to do business because people will already know and will have seen your brand. Your brand will sell itself. You don't have to do much convincing about your product. Your brand does it automatically. There are so many ways to get branded, and you need to determine what is going to work for you and your budget. Branding does not have to be expensive.

The first branding we did was to brand my Nissan 200NP that I had in 2012. In South Africa, we call it a bakkie, and in other countries, it is referred to as a truck or pick-up van. We branded the sides and the back with our logo—large and bold—and on each side, we placed a beautiful picture of a man and a woman. Our slogan and contact details were placed on the rear. Wow, you should have seen people's reactions. There goes the lube van! The result of that branding opened many opportunities for me to talk about my product. People were always curious what kind of lube I was selling. And, of course, I never drove around without samples and stock. I made many a sale alongside the road.

We also teamed up by sponsoring some fitness events like the Battle of the Titans[19] and the Divas Extravaganza, with which I was involved for three years. These events provided great brand credibility, and my brand was and is associated with the health and fitness industry. We did banners, branded

---

19   Battle of the Titans – fitness event, www.battleofthetitans.co.za

sport bags, water bottles, gym towels, and branded caps. We then asked the winners of these prizes to keep on posting the photos on social media. Again, great brand exposure and credibility.

We got branded pens, notebooks, and golf shirts that we handed out to some of our most valuable customers. Another aspect we practice is consistency with our branding message on all social media platforms and in print media. We had fun and gained exposure with the Cape Town 10s, where we sponsored a rugby team, branded their clothing, and handed out a lot of samples around the rugby field and in the beer tent!

The power of effective branding lies in that you don't have to convince people to buy your product. Your product sells itself because it has become a power brand.

With branding, you have two different brands. You have your business brand, and you have your personal brand. Most entrepreneurs make the mistake of integrating the two. Huge mistake. You need to separate yourself from your business brand.

Effective branding requires a strong, powerful brand message. How? By truthfully answering the following five questions:

1. What is your brand vision?
2. Who are you? (Not just your name, but who you really are.)
3. Where do you want to go?

4. What values drive your brand? (i.e. loyalty, authenticity, family, integrity, friendship.)
5. Are you consistent with your brand message? (Think Coca-Cola.)

Personal brand

I always thought that to have a personal brand you must be a celebrity. How wrong and naïve (if at all).

Your personal brand is who you are. It includes your characteristics. It is what you want people to remember and say when you're not around. It's your core value system. How can people know who you really are and what you do if you don't tell them and show them? You need to become the authority in your field. Your personal brand is what sets you apart from your competition. It is what makes you stand out and is the one determining factor as to why people want to do business with you. You should make use of every opportunity to tell people about this. Take as many pictures as you can and post them on social media (but keep them interesting). However, be careful what you post on social media. Your personal brand is ultimately your image, and what you want people to say and think about you. Remember, you control your personal brand. You are your own CEO.

To develop your personal brand, you must ask yourself the following nine important questions:

- Who am I?
- What is it I do?
- What is my vision?

- What is my Why?
- How am I going to market my personal brand?
- What hashtags am I going to consistently use so that more people can recognize and follow me as a brand?
- What are my core values?
- Who am I taking with me?
- What is my goal?

I believe that this is probably one of the most important, yet overlooked, aspects of being a successful entrepreneur. The ability to understand who you are as a person. There was a stage in my life when I truly thought I knew who I was. I mean, I had my title, I was on top of my game, and I made lots of money—until that week at a convention in Los Angeles. Suddenly, I felt lost. I felt that I did not belong among all these amazing successful entrepreneurs and, for the first time in my life, I truly was at a loss for words. This was a very scary, yet eye-opening, moment in my life.

After a few months with my coach, and many frustrations later, I managed to turn this negative experience into a positive one, while learning and understanding more about myself. This involved some deep soul searching, and I had to keep asking myself quality questions. I was determined to find my true self, who I was as a person and entrepreneur. I was also determined to find out exactly what I was bringing to this world. We all have titles to describe what it is we are doing. For instance, "I am a serial entrepreneur." So, what? Many people are. It is just a title. You need to dig very deep. Imagine you are drilling for water. At first you get a few drops, and you think you have hit the jackpot, only to realize that amount is not enough. You must drill deeper and deeper until you hit the spot where the water shoots up into the heavens. That is when you finally hit the jackpot. This is what you must do when you're searching for who you truly are as an entrepreneur. Your jackpot will be when you can answer this question without any doubts in your heart and mind—to anyone in any given situation.

To help you get started on developing your personal brand, and to make it easier for you, I am going to give you my personal example.

Who I am

I am focused, confident, tenacious, energetic, and determined to succeed in everything I do. I am inspirational, motivational, a business strategist, and problem solver.

What do I do?

I restore confidence, happiness, and satisfaction back into people's lives. I am the solutions guy to better people's personal lives through my product brands Lubrimaxxx, Communimail and Erabella Hair Extensions. When they are happy and satisfied in their personal lives, they automatically will thrive in their businesses.

What is my vision and goal?

My vision is to inspire and motivate people to take immediate action for their own success and destiny.

What is my Why?

I want to establish myself as an internationally recognized inspirational speaker and business coach. I want to create credibility to sell my books and training programs. I want to travel the world, and I want to generate some extra income that will enable my family and me to be more financially free to do whatever we want, when, and where we want. Furthermore, I truly want to give people products that will improve their lives and increase their self-confidence.

How am I going to market my personal brand?

I will outsource my public relations and marketing. I will do regular webinars, blogs, and various social media handles to ensure that my brand message reaches my desired target audience.

What hashtags am I going to use?

#coach-karl, #publicspeaking #inspirationalspeaking, #meetkarelvermeulen, #platformspeaker #321Action, #YourResultsOurSuccess,#me,#followme,#pictureofthedays, #motivational, #transformational, #confident, #happiness, #choice.

Do not copy this. This is just an example. Remember you are unique and special. Create your own.

Celebrity branding

You may not care about celebrities but, believe me, many people out there do. Look how the media is flooded with anything a celebrity does, and it sells big time. Celebrity branding is powerful.

In February 2017, I was interviewed on stage in front of 1500 people. I got a lot of photos from that interview. I posted these photos on all my social media platforms, and the response was absolutely mind blowing to say the least. I got my first magazine and radio interviews from those photos. People approached me for photos, and others contacted me about the possibilities of getting Lubrimaxxx in their respective countries. Do you see how powerful this can be?

Use every opportunity to take photos with a celebrity, a well-known person, and even a speaker at an event. You never know who is looking at your picture, and that might open some huge opportunities for you. It does not matter if you only spent a few seconds with that person. The message you want to put out there is that if a well-known person is with you, then you must be worthy to know and do business with.

One major milestone was when I interviewed the famous A-list actor John Travolta in front of 2500 people in Los Angeles in November 2017. Wow! As you can imagine that this experience blew my mind and one that I will never forget. Not do I have the pictures but also the recorded interview that contributes to immense credibility for my personal and business brand.

We cannot control what other people think or assume, but we can control what we give them to form an opinion about.

LESSONS LEARNED

- Your USP (Unique Selling Proposition) sets you apart from your competitors
- It is what differentiates you from your competitor
- It is what your clients/customers say about you and your product when you are not in the room
- Set aside some quality time to understand who you are and what you bring to your customers

Exercise 2.

Who is your ideal customer? List all the attributes. Be specific.

_____

_____

_____

_____

_____

What is the pain that your product or service eliminates?

_____

_____

_____

_____

_____

What is your USP? (Unique Selling Proposition)

_____

_____

_____

_____

_____

What have you done to get branded?

_____

_____

_____

_____

_____

Who are you as your personal brand?

_____

_____

_____

_____

_____

What is your brand vision and mission?

_____

_____

_____

_____

_____

Make a list of events in your area where you can attend and can take photos.

_____

_____

_____

_____

_____

CHAPTER 3

ACCELERATE YOUR SALES
Pricing and Strategy

Now that I knew my angle to get into the market, my next challenge was to determine the correct pricing strategy for my product. I had no idea where to start, so off I went to compare prices at various retailers as well as online. As they say, compare apples to apples. It was quite a challenging process because my product was not the same as those of my competitors.

To get to my pricing strategy, I had to determine my business model by answering the following six questions:

1. Do I want to go for quantity or quality?
2. Who is my target market?
3. Do I want to cater for the low-end, medium or high-end market?
4. What is my production capacity?
5. Am I going to sell to the end consumer, directly to retailers, or just distributors?

6. Am I going to have representatives who will sell to retailers?

It took some serious thinking, but once I truthfully answered all these questions, my pricing structure and business model became easy to follow.

Strange as it may seem, I hated sales at that stage. I read many sales books and listened to sales seminar coaches, but for some reason, I just could not get myself to be passionate about it. There was a big revelation. Why did I hate sales? Because I doubted myself and did not understand what the core of sales was all about. I had to embrace the idea that sales is not a dirty word. Sales is a game and I had to change my mindset to get my sales game face on.

What does this mean?

1. Find a customer and put them in your pipeline.
2. Pitch your product or service to him.
3. Ask them exactly what it is they want and need.
4. Once you know what your customer exact needs and wants are then it is easy to develop the perfect solution for them.
5. For continues sales you then must develop ancillary products.

Here is a fundamental shocking truth: Nobody likes to be sold to, but everybody likes to buy!

Sales are all about finding out what people want and then give it to them. People buy more with emotions than with their minds (common sense). Ask yourself what emotional feeling your product or service satisfies. You'll have to think very hard about this. I also had to dig very deep into my product to get to the emotional pain points that my product, Lubrimaxxx, satisfies.

Now, Lubrimaxxx is a personal lubricant. It is a sex lubricant like Durex or K-Y Jelly. We identified the following pain points, and we addressed these in all our marketing with great success:

LUBRIMAXXX PAIN POINTS

- Fear of painful sex
- Fear of rejection
- Fear of Sexual Transmitted Diseases (STDs)
- Loss of libido (men)
- Low self-esteem
- Low self-confidence
- Fear of not satisfying your partner

Once you have identified that your product or service's specific emotional pain points, are eliminated, your marketing and branding message becomes crystal clear, and you will see an increase in your sales. The message you send out to your clients or customers is one of care.

There are so many aspects to effective salesmanship that I could write many books about them.

Here are fifteen facts I've found to be true and effective:

SALES SUMMARY

- You must believe in yourself first, and only then your product or service.
- Be genuine.
- Nobody likes to be sold to, but everyone likes to buy.
- First impressions are lasting impressions. What is your dress code?
- Smile! It goes a long way.
- The focus is not on you but on your client's emotional needs.
- Communication: practice your introduction. How you introduce yourself in the first twenty-nine seconds will either make or break your sale.
- Attitude is contagious. What's your attitude in front of your client?
- Be authentic. Do not try to be someone you are not.
- Be sincere. Nobody likes to be lied to.
- Care. Show that you are interested in the other person.
- Never over-promise and under-deliver.
- Determine your big WHY. Why must they buy from you? What sets you apart from your competitors?

- Do not be afraid to fail. Failure only occurs when you decide to quit. You choose your results.
- It's not who you know, but WHO KNOWS YOU!

LESSONS LEARNED

- Determine your business model.
- Clarify your target market.
- Determine your product price based on these important questions, truthfully answered.
- Sales is about YOU, not just the product. Who knows and likes you?
- Effective communication is key. Practice your introduction.

Six steps on how to win in business[20]

It is all about strategy!

1. Know the outcome you want before taking any steps.
2. Be ready for objections and have them all covered.
3. Emphasize giving value and how the customer would benefit.
4. Know the facts and numbers.
5. Be confident in your approach.

---

20   Erna Basson: Six Steps on how to win in business

6. Get a business coach.

Speed of Implementation

I was very excited. I just received a quote to ship our products to Dubai. This enormous order would bring me about twelve million rand, a bit over one million US dollars, in the pocket. I immediately started to work on the numbers, and contacted all parties involved to get their numbers to correctly identify my selling price.

I waited and waited to get the numbers from external parties. It was incredibly frustrating. Eventually, when I finally got all the numbers and made my pitch, I was too late. They simply told me, and I quote, "Sorry, we went with someone else because you took too long to give us your numbers."

Boy, oh, boy, was I angry and disappointed. I really needed the money, and because some parties involved were a bit slow in providing me with the figures I needed, I lost out on a potentially huge deal!

Now, we must establish 'quality test' questions. You want your contact to engage with you, and the moment they respond, you need to make sure you keep their attention and curiosity.

LESSONS LEARNED

- Speed of implementation is crucial for success.
- Do not rely on other parties. Keep on pushing and nagging until you get the desired result.
- I can only blame myself for not getting the desired results.
- Never assume the other party will understand the urgency of an order You have to drill that into them.
- Plan for the worst and the best outcomes

Exercise 3.

Evaluate your pricing structure. Are you in line with your market?

_____
_____
_____
_____
_____

Why must your customers buy from you? What is your big WHY?

_____
_____
_____

_____

_____

How visible are you? Does your customer know about you, and how?

_____

_____

_____

_____

_____

Can you introduce yourself in twenty-nine seconds? Write down your introductory pitch. No longer than seventeen words.

_____

_____

_____

_____

_____

_____

_____

CHAPTER 4

ALL ABOUT MINDSET

My mind is always busy—always thinking ahead, with so many things at the same time, it seems I'm talking to myself. If someone had to record my thoughts, they would think that I had lost the plot and needed to be admitted to a psychiatric institution.

To the outside world, I seem a positive person who is completely in control. This was not always the case. You see, I will be the first to admit that, even today, I still struggle with signs of depression, loneliness, destructive thoughts, anger, and even doubts in myself. Yes, despite my success. One thing I pride myself on is that when I get these thoughts and feelings, I'll ponder over them for a day or two, feel sorry for myself, and then, miraculously, I'll get myself out of it! This is an effective coping mechanism I've learned over the years.

How do I do that? I utilize the power of my mind by talking positively to myself. Let me give you an example:

When I am in a state of depression, I will, at some point, begin telling myself the following: *Karel, this is not worth it. I am much better than this. This is not going to win the battle to defeat me. I must pick myself up–no one is going to do this for me. This state I am in is not doing anybody any good. Put on your big boy pants. I must earn a living, and if I do not pick myself up and get out of this situation, I will not have money to pay my debts and enjoy a good living!*

You see, it's a positive method of self-talk and, I must say, it's amazing when you start doing this, how your mind begins to believe it, and how the situation changes. We all have our struggles and down days. It is all about what you are doing with those days. Are you lying in self-pity all the time, or are you going to pick yourself up, wipe away your tears, and become a stronger, better person and learn from it?

I am a strong self-motivator. I had to learn that from a very young age; I had no one who believed in me or encouraged me to be a success. I believe that motivation does not come from outside forces or circumstances. How many times have you been to a motivational speaker, felt inspired to go and change your situation or world, and a few days later, you're still where you were before you went to the event?

It all starts between your ears. Your belief system. What do you believe to be true about yourself? You can only act out what you believe. As the saying goes: Whatever you believe to be true in a certain situation–that is true to you.

Your beliefs provide your motivation, and together with your motivation, hard, smart work, and discipline (habits), you will get your desired results. Don't get me wrong. You can't simply believe and expect that magic will happen. You need to be true to yourself, accept where you are, and begin to act accordingly. No actions–no results!

Have you heard the saying that your attitude determines your altitude? I'm sure you have. "Attitude drives actions. Actions drive results. Results drive lifestyles." This quote is from American business philosopher, Jim Rohn.[21] Our minds are extremely powerful. Everything starts with a thought planted as a seed. It is up to you to water that seed, so that it grows into a plant, by being mindful about that thought and acting accordingly. The choice is up to you whether you want to learn how to use more of your mind power or not.

My life completely turned 180 degrees for the better in 2011, when I attended a mind power seminar. I immediately started implementing some of the very basic principles. I was blown away to realize what a huge influence my mind had on my actions and my belief system.

I did, however, walk out of that seminar, because at that specific moment in time, the way the seminar was conducted was not what I needed. My mindset and emotions were not in line to accept the truth about what they were teaching. Although I walked out, this extremely powerful affirmation stuck in my mind:

> *"My thoughts, my words, and my actions are powerful forces of attraction."*[22]

It was a shock to my system when I had to admit to myself that I was the reason I was not successful, and that money

---

21 America's Business Philosopher, www.jimrohn.com
22 Mind Power into the 21st Century, John Kehoe

was not coming into my life as I thought it would–that I was the reason why so many negative things were happening in my life, all because of my programmed negative thinking and the negative words I spoke about myself. Subconsciously, I programmed my mind to attract all these bad and negative results in my life. Wow, what a shocker and eye-opener it was. So, what did I do? I started to write down some positive affirmations that I would say out loud to myself daily. Even when I did not believe them I continued to say them to myself, always expressing positivity, as if they were already true, I must admit that it was not easy, but the more I did it, the easier it became for me to believe. I even recorded it on my phone, so that I could listen to it while walking on the beach and while falling asleep.

One of the most important truths I learned was "that I am worthy enough" to have whatever my heart desires and the universe wants to give me. The important aspect here is not to look for a reason why you are worthy enough. When you do that, you'll find a limited belief in your mind, and you'll automatically want to find a reason why you're not worthy enough. The fact that I am alive today is reason enough to make me worthy to have all that my heart desires and have all my dreams come true.

A comfort zone is never a good place or state of mind to find yourself in. There is no growth in a comfort zone. It is a zone of safety, of complacency, of comfort and certainly no financial growth. The following are some characteristics of being in a comfort zone:

- A dull life
- Fear
- Procrastination
- Just getting by
- Playing it safe
- Feeling regret
- Being like everyone else
- Surviving
- Settling for less

The important question you must ask yourself is whether you want to be like the 98% of the population living in a comfort zone or do you want to be like the few 2% who are in control of their mindset while experiencing the following:

- Confidence
- Happiness
- Fulfillment
- Excitement
- Abundance
- Living without limits
- Going after their dreams
- Embracing the unknown
- Liking change
- Act despite fear
- Joy

Let me give you some examples to help you create your own worthy and positive affirmations:

I AM WORTHY

- I am worthy to have all my dreams come true.
- I am worthy to be loved and to love.
- I am worthy to be successful in everything I do.
- I am worthy to wear beautiful clothes.
- I am worthy to have my own house.
- I am worthy to have all my financial needs met.
- I am worthy to drive an expensive car.
- I am worthy to have beautiful furniture.
- I am worthy to be happy.
- I am worthy to go on regular getaways and vacations.

MY POSITIVE AFFIRMATIONS

- I am a highly successful strategic business entrepreneur.
- I am self-motivated.
- I am a great product developer.
- I am a self-starter.
- I am friendly and generous.
- I am financially free and deserve to earn $_____ per month. (You decide what amount of money you want to earn per month and add it in.)
- I am tenacious.
- I am prosperous in everything I do.
- I am responsible for my own success.
- I am healthy, fit, lean, and masculine.
- I am a smart and hard worker.
- I am a great listener.
- I am a passionate and great inspirational speaker.
- I am happy.
- I am calm, focused, determined, and I achieve my goals.

You see what I'm doing here? Now you do the same. Start right now, and write your own *Worthy and Positive Affirmation List.* Then repeat it every single day until it becomes part of you.

I learned to love to work out in the gym or go for a run in the forest. There were many times, I did not feel like working out, but once I started and finished I felt refreshed and energized. In the beginning it was not easy but as I persist it became second nature. I had to force myself many times just to get out of bed. This morning ritual became a habit and now it is very easy for me to get myself to do some sort of physical activity. Now I reap the reward of a healthy and fit body.

Just like our muscles need to be trained on a regular basis, so you must train your mind regularly to stay mentally fit and strong. You can accomplish anything that you set your mind to. You can be whoever you want to be. Oprah, Richard Branson, Ray Croc (McDonald's) and many more highly successful individuals were often up against high odds and with determination became a success. Some of these individuals became a success later in life (Colonel Sanders of KFC Chicken was 62 when he first franchised his now world-famous chicken), but they never gave up and their passion and actions turned them into a major successful figure. If it can happen to them it can happen to you. They defied the odds and made it happen. If they can do, so can you.

What you require is a strong belief that you deserve it as much as anyone else. You will be like a magnet. You will begin to attract the right opportunities and people who can get you there. Some will succeed faster than others and some will succeed much easier than others, but we all have the chance to succeed no matter what circumstances we face.

12 STEPS OF HOW TO BE MENTALLY STRONG

- Don't fear alone time
- Don't dwell on the past
- Don't feel the world owes you
- Don't expect immediate results
- Don't waste time feeling sorry for yourself
- Don't worry about pleasing everyone
- Don't waste energy on things you can't control
- Don't let others influence your emotions
- Don't resent other people's success
- Don't' shy away from responsibilities
- Don't give up after the first failure
- Don't fear taking calculated risks

How you change is how you succeed. How can you expect to have better or different results if you repeatedly do the same things, thinking you will have a better outcome? Get out of your comfort zone, challenge yourself, and you will be amazed to see and experience positive results.

I love the statement from Kerwin Rae: "In order for you to hit that next level, for you to grow in your business, the fact remains that you must be willing to grow. And growth equals discomfort."[23]

---

23   Kerwin Rae, www.kerwinrae.com

We need to learn to be comfortable by being uncomfortable. I know this is not a good place to be, but believe me, it is worth it. Again, what is your mindset?

Learn to love discomfort. Embrace it as your friend. We need to change and adjust our thinking. Not everything we think is bad, actually is bad for us. It is there to serve us, to guide us, and to enlighten us to grow. Discomfort in business will not kill you. But it will make you a whole lot stronger. Discomfort is good!

LESSONS LEARNED

- Never underestimate the power of your mind.
- Practice daily positive affirmations.
- It's okay to feel down or have a bad day. Pick yourself up.
- You are your greatest motivator.
- Learn to be comfortable by being uncomfortable.

Strategic Thinking

One of the biggest mistakes I made when I started Lubrimaxxx was not to have a strategic plan for my sales and growth. I took each day as it came. I spent most of my day going through emails, writing a business plan, being on social media to see how I could communicate the brand effectively, and doing all the admin chores. While I was working for myself, and felt pretty good about it, I was a slave to my own business. Wow! And there I was thinking that I was an entrepreneur, yet, working as if I was no better off than any employee at a company.

I was working IN my businesses instead of ON my business. This realization was a huge wake-up call.

As successful entrepreneurs, we should be working ON our business instead of IN our business. What does that mean? Working in your business is dealing with the daily operational and admin tasks, while working on your business is creating the strategies, ideas, and vision, and then getting your staff to implement them. Strategic thinking and mindfulness go together. They are like twins. If you fail to plan, you plan to fail. It is as simple as that.

Vision + Mission + Goals + Strategy = Results & Success.

Vision

At Lubrimaxxx, we want to become the world's leading sexual health product brand. What is your vision for your company?

As a public speaker, my vision is to be invited to share the stage with the biggest and most influential public platform speakers. This way, I can inspire and empower people to take #321 action for their own lives, happiness, and growth.

Mission

My mission with Lubrimaxxx is to change people's perceptions and thinking around using personal lubricants.

This we do by creating healthy conversation between people. Your mission is the steps that you must take in order to to accomplish your vision. This is the HOW in which you are going to do things.

My mission with my public speaking is to empower, inspire, and motivate one million people to take #321 action and responsibility for their lives, happiness and growth.

Goals

Goals need to be realistic and measurable. There must be a time frame with each goal. It's important that you're clear on your goals. Many people say they want to be healthy or lose weight. That is not a clear goal. "I want to lose twenty pounds within the next six months." is a measurable, clear-cut goal. Get the point?

For every goal, you need to write out your strategy.

How do you strategize?

Here is my eight-point strategic planning process map that you can incorporate in any situation.

STRATEGIC PLANNING PROCESS

- Evaluate each situation.
- Identify the negative patterns/habits.
- Determine your clear-cut goal(s)/vision.
- Reverse engineer the process from your goal(s)/ vision, breaking down what you need to do to achieve this step by step.

- Write down all the action steps with a dedicated time frame.
- Implement your plan of action.
- Get someone outside your business to hold you accountable.
- Evaluate the progress.

Time Management

I used to be very bad at time management. I sucked at it big time. Due to my active mind, I was easily distracted. I tend to do the things I love first and put off the lesser things only to find out that I hardly get around to them. Do you know what I am talking about? Of course, you do. There are so many teachings out there on how to manage your time more effectively and, believe me, I have tried many of them. Most of these did not work for me. Until I learned that it is not time management that is the problem, but it is how we manage our energy. You see, time is there, and there is nothing that we can do about it. But what we can do is manage our energy around the time factor, which makes such a big difference.

Jeffrey Gitomer[24] mentions that lessons in time management are pretty much a waste of time, and what we need are lessons in procrastination.

It is all about asking ourselves questions like "What is important right now?" and "How do we do this?" Create

---

24 Jeffrey Gilbert, Little Red Book of Selling, p.45

a Not-To-Do list and a To-Do list on one sheet of paper. Under the Not-To-Do list, write all the things you need to stop doing that are wasting your time.

MY NOT-TO-DO LIST

- Stop saying *I can't*.
- Stop all negative self-talk.
- Stop checking my emails first thing in the morning.
- Stop checking my phone every time I hear a beep.
- Stop complaining.

LESSONS LEARNED

- Plan your day in advance.
- Create your Not-To-Do list.
- Create your To-Do list.
- Effective time management is all about effective energy management.
- To be the BEST you can be for others, you must first be the BEST for yourself.
- Define your personal and core business values.
- Most of the time, when we struggle with "time management," it means that our core values are

not clearly defined or in line with our purpose, vision, and goals.

Exercise 4.

How do you stay motivated on a bad day?

_____

_____

_____

_____

_____

Write down at least ten positive affirmations that you will practice for the next thirty days.

_____

_____

_____

_____

_____

Review your vision, mission, and goals. Write them and communicate them to your staff.

_____

_____

_____

_____

_____

Create your Not-To-Do list.

_____

_____

_____

_____

_____

_____

_____

_____

_____

CHAPTER 5

THE NAKED TRUTH

Why do you want to become an entrepreneur?

This may come as a shock, but to be brutally honest, if I knew what I know today when I ventured out to become an entrepreneur, I probably would not have made that decision.

The reason I'm making this bold statement is because there's hardly a person out there with balls enough (excuse my language) to tell you what it takes to become a successful entrepreneur. Most paint a picture of how great and excellent it is to be your own boss. BS. Becoming an entrepreneur, let alone a successful one, is not an easy, happy-go-lucky venture.

It is damned hard, with lots of frustration, late nights, loneliness, hard work, tears, and sweat. Oh, and then you still must deal with taxes, company registrations, employees, and industry specific regulations.

Okay, I know I sound negative now. Let me put your mind at ease. I love being an entrepreneur. I'm glad I didn't know these things in advance. I learn every single day, and that makes me a stronger person. I doubt that I'll ever be working for a boss again.

I believe that we live in very uncertain times. Uncertain about our job security, uncertain about our lives in general, and uncertain where our current economy is heading. Let's face it, those thoughts can be scary. What is the answer? Should we all venture out, take a leap of faith, and become entrepreneurs?

> **Entrepreneur:** *"A person who organizes and operates a business, taking on greater-than-normal financial risks to do so."*

I believe that most people have the ability to become entrepreneurs. Some, however, will be better at it than others, but it is simply a skill that can be learned. You need to identify the important characteristics of an entrepreneur and work at improving these skills if they don't already come naturally to you.

I love what Tim Ferriss says about an entrepreneur: *"An entrepreneur isn't someone who owns a business. It's someone who make things happen."*

As in all aspects of life, we need balance. We need doctors, nurses, firemen, law enforcement, lawyers, dentists, librarians, administrative workers, and so on. They each have an important function in keeping our society balanced.

Not all people are born entrepreneurs or want to become entrepreneurs. Being an entrepreneur isn't always as easy as it sounds or as glamorous as it looks. It is a hard and sometimes a lonely road to success.

FIVE MOST COMMON PSYCHOLOGICAL CHALLENGES

- Most of the time, you handle stress alone.
- You will experience numerous moments of failures.
- You may have to fire some of your friends.
- You may struggle to balance work and personal life.
- You will experience constant market pressure.

WHAT ARE THE CHARACTERISTICS OF AN ENTREPRENEUR?

- Willing to take calculated risks (not gambling).
- Must be prepared to move out of your comfort zone.
- Able to problem-solve using logic, intuition, and experience.
- In most cases, you need to be a "people" person.
- Have plenty of self-discipline. Remember, there will be no boss to make you work.

- Willingness to continue learning and developing new skills.
- Have a general understanding as to how the business world works.
- Strongly self-motivated. There will be many tough times ahead.
- Be coachable. You will not have all the answers, even if you think you do.

I believe this is a great time for young entrepreneurs to rise up, take their place in the business world, and create their own financial freedom. The spirit of entrepreneurship is alive and well.

THE INEVITABLES OF AN ENTREPRENEUR

- You will feel pain
- You will cry before you get it
- You will lose some of your friends
- You will doubt yourself thousands of times
- You will develop weird habits
- You will lose money
- Your family will discourage you
- You will think you're going crazy
- People will hate you for no reason
- You will almost talk yourself out of it hundreds of times
- It will all be worth it

LESSONS LEARNED

- Find your WHY.
- Know that you are not alone in this struggle.
- Find healthy outlets for relieving stress and gaining perspective on setbacks.
- Reach out to other entrepreneur–networks.

Exercise 5.

Why did you become an entrepreneur?

_____

_____

_____

_____

_____

Write down the network groups that you currently belong to or are planning to attend and why they are relevant.

_____

_____

_____

_____

_____

Write down how you deal with and handle stress.

_____

_____

_____

_____

_____

CHAPTER 6

POWER TO EMPOWER

Take back your power and rule your world.

Empowerment is the authority or power given to someone to do something. In no way should this authority be misused in a negative way.

What I want to focus on is self-empowerment. For most of my life, I thought I couldn't do much, that I couldn't be successful. Throughout my school days, I was verbally and physically bullied for being different. For not being like the other boys in school, as I mentioned earlier. This had a tremendous impact on my life while growing up. This explains that, even in work, I didn't excel, as I should have, and in my personal relationships, the feeling of being different had the same effect. I felt insecure while silently, constantly fighting the "depression demon." At times, I even lashed out in personally destructive behavior.

Later in my life, I was so down and out, tired of living, and unable to achieve any success (both financially and in my personal relationships) that, out of desperation, I went to a Robin Banks *Mind Power*[25] seminar in Cape Town. I took two things away from those seminars. First, I bought John Kehoe's book, *Mind Power into the 21st Century*, with Robin's foreword, and next, these unforgettable words stuck in my head: "My thoughts, my words, and my actions are powerful forces of attraction." I started to read this book, and every day I would say positive affirmations out loud, even when I did not believe them. Amazingly, my mindset and my life started to change for the better. Our subconscious mind does not know the difference between reality or fiction. We become what we feed our minds. You become the sum of the five people you spend the most time with. What you believe and tell yourself—that is true to you.

We all know the law of gravity. If you're on planet earth, you're bound by its laws, whether you believe in them or not. The universe also has its own laws. One principal law is that we attract what we believe, consciously or subconsciously. I've learned and experienced that our minds and words are very powerful, and often prophetic. Whatever you believe at a certain time in your life, no matter what other people tell you, is true to you. A quote that is so true by Napoleon Hill: "Whatever the mind can conceive and believe, the mind can achieve."

---

25   Robin Banks, Mind Power Seminars, www.robinbanks.co.za

Self-Empowerment

We are all responsible for our own lives, our own happiness, and our own success. How do we do that? Look at this figure and let me explain:

In mathematics, the triangle is a very strong shape. Stronger than a circle, a square, or rectangle. The big A stands for Action. The three important steps you need for self-improvement are:

1. Take control of your own life.
2. Set achievable goals.
3. Make positive choices.

Remember: The way you change is the way you succeed. I also learned that not everyone you meet, even your closest friends or family, would like you to succeed or get ahead in life. Be very careful with whom you share your goals and dreams.

Myths

- When the time is right, it will happen.
- God willing, it will happen.
- What will be will be.
- I can't.

Ten Tips for self-empowerment

Here are my ten tips to help you with your self-empowerment. These worked for me on many occasions:

1. Practice mindfulness daily.
2. Stop all negative, self-destructive talk.
3. Practice daily positive self-affirmations.
4. Get a coach.
5. Create a Not-To-Do list and a To-Do list.
6. Surround yourself with people who believe in you.
7. Believe that you are worthy enough.
8. Love yourself.
9. Practice daily gratitude.
10. Forgive yourself.

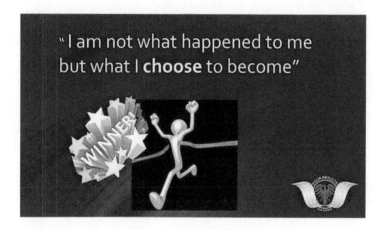

" I am not what happened to me but what I **choose** to become"

Learn to trust your gut—your intuition

I am so excited! It is June 2013 and I have an appointment with two gentlemen from two major retail chain stores who are coming to my new warehouse to discuss the possibility of getting Lubrimaxxx into their stores. Wow, this will be a first, and just what I need to get my name out there. Or so I thought.

They arrived in a black Bentley, dressed in suits. From the start, they dominated the conversation, hardly giving me time to talk. This made me very uncomfortable, and for some reason, I didn't have a good feeling about this meeting. "Stop it, Karel. You are just over-analyzing and emotional," I told myself. Then came the final nail in the coffin. They wanted my product in their packaging, but my name and product were not allowed on their packaging. It was then I knew it was not going to work. I had to dig deep, weighing the pros and cons. Their reactions when I told them that I was building my own brand, and what they were proposing was not going to work, confirmed what I was sensing, and feeling were true, and that I made the right decision. They told me that I would never make it in the business, and that I would never build a brand name. Well, I proved them wrong on so many levels.

We must learn to trust our gut feelings. That inner voice inside each of us is our friend. It is that feeling or sense you get when something is not what it seems. Some call it intuition or sixth sense. I believe they are all the same, so use the term that resonates best with you. Our gut feeling is there to protect us. Learn to listen, and trust that feeling.

On the other hand, the opposite is also true. I learned again a hard and valuable lesson when I did not trust my gut feeling and went with what seemed to be the obvious or emotional decision.

I had a bodybuilder come to me for some financial help with his business. I knew him for a while, and he told me such an emotional story about his business, failures, and struggles to keep his family together that I got emotionally swept up. My inner voice screamed at me not to give him money, but because I was so emotional, I ignored that inner voice and gut feeling and loaned him the money. To this day, he still owes me almost $10,000, not to mention attorney fees.

Will I listen to my inner voice and gut feeling from now on? You bet I will!

What does your gut feeling, or inner voice tell you about your business? This will be one of the greatest and most important things you'll need to learn in business. Learn, develop, and practice to trust your gut and intuition.

LESSONS LEARNED

- Learn to trust your gut feeling/inner voice.
- You are either your worst enemy, or you can be your best sounding board.

Exercise 6.

What in your personal life is holding you back from reaching your full potential?

_____

_____

_____

_____

_____

Stand in front of your mirror, strip naked, then look in the mirror and tell yourself that you love yourself.

What are your achievable goals for the next thirty, sixty, and ninety days? Be specific.

Thirty Days:

_____

_____

_____

_____

_____

Sixty Days:

_____

_____

_____

_____

_____

Ninety Days:

_____

_____

_____

_____

_____

Be attentive to your gut feeling/inner voice. Write down that feeling. After you give it some attention, write down the outcome.

_____

_____

_____

_____

_____

CHAPTER 7

EFFECTIVE NETWORKING

Sometimes in life, you have to do things that you don't really want, but you must. Networking was one of these nightmares for me. I used to dread going to networking events.

I would be the guy who was constantly busy on his cell phone—pretending to be talking to someone or checking my mail, all in an attempt to avoid talking to strangers. Today, I know why I did that. I was afraid of talking to other people simply because I did not know what to say or how to network effectively.

After I joined the Intelligent Millionaires Network (IMN) in October 2016, I learned the value of quality networking and what it can do for my personal life, confidence, and my business today, I love networking.

Your network equals your net worth.

How incredible is this statement?

Networking is life skills and social skills combined with sales skills. Networking is a mandatory function of business for salespeople and entrepreneurs. The more "high-quality people" your network consists of, the more you can monetize it. Networking can and should be fun. To get the most out of networking, you need to know how to communicate effectively in a very short period (about twenty-nine seconds). This includes who you are, what business you're in, and what you are looking for, as well as the value you can give to the other person. It's not just about you but, more important, it's the value that you bring to the other party that makes you stand out.

It takes one person and one deal to change your life forever and for good. You never know who you'll meet at a networking event. In August 2017, I attended a three-day event in Johannesburg. There, I networked with a lot of people. I met this one woman from Dubai, we connected, exchanged business cards, and went for dinner three days later. We discussed opportunities for my business to get into the Dubai market because she knew most of the appropriate people and procedures. You see, the power of networking can open many wonderful doors for you.

My seven steps to successful networking:

STEPS TO SUCCESSFUL NETWORKING

- Learn and practice your twenty-nine-second introduction.
- Have a clear goal as to why you are going to the networking event.

- Decide beforehand how many people you want to talk to.
- Keep it simple-less is more.
- Mindset: What value can I give the other person?
- Exchange business cards when you are connecting.
- Follow up with each person you exchanged business cards with within forty-eight hours.

Here are the The Seven Principles of Networking as laid out by Jeffrey Gitomer,[26]

To understand quality networking, we need to understand the fundamental principles of why we network. For any networking to work, you need to know the two-word secret: Show up!

PRINCIPLES OF NETWORKING

- To get known by those who count.
- To get more prospects.
- To make more contacts.
- To make more sales.
- To build quality relationships.
- To make a career advancement (or just get a job).

---

26 *Little Red Book of Selling* by Jeffrey Gitomer, p.85.

- To build your reputation (and be seen and known as consistent).

Your twenty-nine-second introduction

Within twenty-nine seconds, you must be able to communicate your name, who you are, what you do, and what you are looking for in about seventeen to twenty-one words. Remember that at most networking events, you have only a couple of minutes to introduce yourself, make an impression, and snag a quality lead.

Example:

Hello, my name Karel Vermeulen. I am a serial entrepreneur, a motivational speaker, business transformation coach, and published author. Is there any area within your business that you struggle and may need help with?.

You see, straight to the point. After your introduction, if the other party is interested, and follows suit, then you can go ahead and dig deeper into the person's business by asking a couple of pertinent questions to determine if you both can add value to one another.

Be prepared. Have a couple of relevant questions ready in your pocket.

SAMPLE POWER NETWORKING QUESTIONS

- Why are you at this networking event?
- What do you need assistance with?

- How can I add value to your business?
- Would you mind exchanging business cards?
- May I contact you within two days?

This is the power of quality networking.

LESSONS LEARNED

- Nobody is born a great networker, but great networking can be learned.
- To grow your network, you should join a nearby network group.
- Plan and research in advance before you go to a networking event.
- You must make initial contact–no one is going to do it for you.
- Always have business cards with you.
- Always follow up no later than forty-eight hours after you contacted people at your networking event.
- Do not always think "What can I get?" out of this networking event. Instead have the mindset of "What can I do for you?"

Exercise 7.

What is your goal when you go to a networking event?

_____

_____

_____

_____

_____

Write your introduction down in specific terms.
Who are you? Start with the words I am…"

_____

_____

_____

_____

_____

What is it you do?

_____

_____

_____

_____

_____

What is the emotional pain you eliminate?

_____

_____

_____

_____

What can you do for the other person? (Be specific)

_____

_____

_____

_____

_____

Write down three to five power questions that you can use
and ask at every networking event.

_____

_____

_____

_____

_____

_____

_____

_____

_____

CHAPTER 8

COACHING IS ESSENTIAL!

Why every entrepreneur needs a business coach

I am, by nature, a very proud person. The need to be proud of who we are and what we do in life, was instilled in me from a very young age by my parents and one of my grandparents. It's a good thing, right? Well, not always, I found. For me it was a case of, "I am very proud, so I am always right." I used to try and do everything myself, hardly ever asking for help. Sometimes in life this works, but most of the times this places a limit on oneself. I remember, as a child, watching martial arts movies such as *The Karate Kid* series, those of Jean-Claude Van Dame, Bruce Lee etc. (some of my childhood heroes). What I loved about those movies was the heroes all had a coach, a trainer who believed in them and would push them beyond their limits. Oh, how I dreamed of having a trainer or coach in my life. I always believed it would remain a fantasy because we were so poor. My lucky break came when I was forty-one, and I had enough money to pay for a personal trainer in the gym—Peter Gaiser from

LBN Fitness Studio. This made me feel like the richest man in the world.

This was my first opportunity to learn about the power of coaching. I previously thought that I trained and ate just fine, but oh boy, was I wrong. You see, a coach will show you where you're making mistakes, show you how to rectify them, and push you when you feel you can't go any further. Look at all the successful athletes today around the world; no matter what sport they participate in, they all have a coach, sometimes even more than one. A coach looks at your life from the outside while keeping your missions and goals in mind. A coach will not feel sorry for you if you make a mistake or do not live up to your goals. A coach is there to guide you to be the best you can. It is crucial to find the correct coach who is in line and compatible with your goals.

Today I have six coaches: a personal trainer and five business coaches. And I am on my way to getting yet another. You use different coaches who specialize in different areas. It is important to define your goals clearly, so you do not waste your money and both your own and your coach's time. The question you must ask yourself is "What will I benefit from this particular coach?" It is important to be honest and upfront with your coach. Remember, a coach can only help you based on the depth of information you share with them. Think about working with a coach in the same way you would when visiting your doctor. If you leave out any symptoms of your illness and what medication you are currently taking, then you risk being wrongly diagnosed, getting the wrong medication, which might, ultimately, cost you your health or worst-case scenario, even your life!

Business coaching, and how it works

Business coaching is not the same as mentoring. A mentor can be a friend who cares about you and your long-term development. A coach, on the other hand, develops specific skills for the task, challenges you, and holds you accountable. A great business coach takes you beyond your excuses, to doing what you know you must to succeed and build wealth better and faster

Mentoring is usually a free two-way mutually beneficial relationship. On the other hand, business coaching is not free–you must pay. A business coach will not only give you guidance, but will, in detail, dive deep into your current business and dissect every little detail to get to the core of the problem in your business or life. A business coach isn't there to tell you what you want to hear and sweet talk you, but to get you to action and results—fast.

How does business coaching work? You can choose from a group session, online coaching, or what I consider the best: one-on-one coaching when and if you can afford it.

How to choose the correct business coach

Each business coach has a field of specialty. Just as professional athletes have many coaches throughout their growth and careers, the same principles apply to entrepreneurs and small business owners.

Here are my seven steps to help you to choose the correct coach.

1. Determine WHY you need a coach.
2. What are your goals? Where do you want to take your business?
3. Identify the areas in which you need immediate help.
4. Ask yourself, and answer truthfully: "Am I coachable?"
5. Assess your financial commitment.
6. Schedule a meeting with the prospective coach, and don't be afraid to ask questions such as: "What is your area of specialty?"
7. Action: Speed of implementation is key. Sign up and grow your business to the next profitable level.

Where to find the ideal coach

In my experience, I would say that it's best to join a business or entrepreneurial network in your area. If you can, join a global network. Usually, in these networking sessions, there are many people who also are business coaches. The alternative is to go online and search for the best business coach in your area. Don't be afraid to ask around, even on social media. Ask your friends or someone who's successful whether they have a coach they can refer to you. Word of mouth is the best referral.

LESSONS LEARNED

- Get a coach.
- A business coach will not smooth talk you into what you want to hear.
- Coaching does not cost you money; it makes you money.

Exercise 8.

List the areas where you are struggling in your business.

_____

_____

_____

_____

_____

_____

_____

What would it mean for you, in your family and business life, if you could get a business coach who could help increase your profits by 30 percent?

_____

_____

_____

_____

_____

Based on your answer above, get yourself a business coach NOW! Write down the name of your business coach.

_____

_____

_____

_____

_____

Some of my coaching clients

CHAPTER 9

START-UP PRINCIPLES

created my first business, Male Wellbeing Therapeutic Treatments, in December 2008, when I moved to Cape Town. I had enough money for a bachelor flat in Sea Point, a few personal items, a bottle of massage oil, and a massage table. I had no formal business training, took the plunge, and went with my gut. This was one of the best decisions I have ever made in my life.

Each month, I barely made it, but I kept pushing on. Three years later, I moved into a two-bedroom flat on the beach in Mouille Point, where I ran my business successfully for another two years. That's where I eventually created Lubrimaxxx personal lubricant in my apartment kitchen.

I knew nothing about business principles, how to register a company, a trademark, accounting, marketing, and branding—not to mention how to develop a product from scratch. I had to learn the hard way, and I basically taught myself. I read as much as I could by getting books and magazines about business principles. Yes, I lost a lot of money in the process as a result of bad business decisions and lack of knowledge, but I learned and got better every day.

My forte was that I was hungry for success and determined to learn whatever and whenever I could. I remember walking so many times, late at night, on Sea Point Promenade, angry at the world, and at God for letting me down. I couldn't get ahead in life. So many times, I wanted to give up on life and myself, but there was that little voice inside that kept on reassuring me that I was destined for something better and bigger than what I was experiencing then. That voice kept me going.

There are so many aspects to business that I could write an enormously thick book on these business principles. This is not what I attempt to do here. In fact, I know you want to get started; therefore, I am going to give you some shortcuts. Is that okay with you?

Before I get to those, it's important to know that it isn't easy, and that you must be willing to fail many times in order to or before you succeed.

Here is my "cheat sheet," or checklist, that will help you tick all the required boxes to succeed in your start-up business.

START-UP CHECKLIST

- Decide on your company name. It must be relevant to your business.
- Decide what you want to do.
- Write down your vision, mission, and goals.

- Register your company with the required agencies.
- Will you be the sole owner of your company?
- If you decide to trademark your product or logo–do so. Remember to do a trademark search first.
- Set up your business email, website, and social media handles (Facebook, Twitter, Instagram, LinkedIn, and others).
- Decide if you are going to work from home or rent office space.
- If you have a product, be sure to do the required product testing.
- Get an accountant and attorney to draw up all legal forms.
- Will you work alone, or are you going to employ staff? If so, on a part-time or full-time basis?
- Register your employees for all relevant legal registrations and legally required benefits.
- Do you want to be VAT (value-added tax) registered?
- Get a business telephone line.
- Get business cards and stationery.
- Draw up supplier contracts.
- Get the required trade licenses.
- Get general insurance and product liability insurance.
- Get a cell phone for business use.
- Draw up your marketing and budget plan.

- Obtain office furniture.
- Determine pricing structures and payment terms.
- Draw up company SOPs (standing operating procedures).
- Develop salary structures.
- Cash flow is king.
- Finances (use personal money or get investors in your business).
- What is your exit strategy? (Is it to work long-term in your business, or do you want to build it into a profitable business, and then sell it?)

CHAPTER 10

HIGHLY SUCCESSFUL ENTREPRENEURS
Tips and Quotes

Robbie and Michael Mathews SERIAL ENTREPRENEURS, CERTIFIED LIFE
COACHES & INTERNATIONAL SPEAKERS

American husband and wife business partners, Michael "Bart" Mathews and Robbie Mathews, are successful entrepreneurs, investors, financial education coaches, celebrity interviewers, and international speakers. Michael also is the author of the book *Financially Speaking: The Best Improvement Starts with Self-Improvement—Create Your Own Economic Stimulus Plan.*

They are advocates for financial literacy education, having shared their messages on stage together with, or in the company of, international leaders and other notables such as Kofi Annan, former Secretary-General of the United Nations, and Nobel Peace Prize recipient; Dr. Ervin Laszlo, twice nominated for the Nobel Peace Prize; Nelson Mandela's grandson, Ndaba Mandela; "The Godfather" himself, Al Pacino; John Travolta; 50Cent; Randi Zuckerberg, former Director of Marketing Development at Facebook; Coach Mike Ditka of the 1985 Chicago Bears NFL Super Bowl Champions; Calvin Klein, fashion designer; and serial entrepreneurs JT Foxx, Damien Elston, and Steve Down.

Michael and Robbie founded the US-based Mathews Entrepreneur Group (TMEG) in 2007. Initially established as a self-publishing book company, TMEG has evolved into a brand committed to empowering people to both "hone" and "own" their personal and small business finances. TMEG specializes in providing financial literacy education, empowerment, accountability, and results-driven strategies using speaking engagements, panel discussions, educational books and CDs, workshops, seminars, and one-on-one accountability, results-driven, personal, or group coaching.

Their mission is "to provide personal financial literacy education, globally." The goal is to give their clients a comprehensive, easy-to-use set of tools, providing them with the knowledge and skills needed to take control of their personal finances, along with achieving and maintaining lifelong financial stability, building a legacy for their children's children, and promoting responsible financial decision-making and consumer spending. "We want to change how people think, act, and feel about their money," they say. "Our motto is 'Educate and Entertain the Planet.'"

In February 2017, Michael spoke in Johannesburg, South Africa to a crowd of well over 1,200 attendees from more than twenty countries across the globe. During his speech, he shared the company's seven "It's okay to be wealthy principles" © as part of their global message on the importance of financial literacy education and the need for change. In addition to Michael delivering an empowering financial literacy education speech, Robbie interviewed Nelson Mandela's grandson, Ndaba Mandela, on stage. Robbie asked Ndaba, "What advice would you give the people of South Africa to help them change from a culture of spending to a culture of saving for their financial future?"

Ndaba Mandela responded by saying, "You must make your family a priority and save for your future. My inspiration is my children and the children across the world."

Michael and Robbie also are committed to giving back both time and money to the global community. They believe becoming successful comes with great responsibility to help others. For years, the couple has donated to the Historically

Black Colleges and Universities Scholarship Fund to help educate and grow future leaders, along with the United Way, Breast Cancer Research, and the American Heart Association. In 2017, they assisted in the relief efforts with the children of South Africa in Hout Bay during the massive fire that placed thousands of families in desperate need.

In addition, their private investments are made with service to others and giving back to the community in mind. They are part of an investment group building two hundred Even Stevens (a Steve Down company) casual sandwich shops across the United States. For every sandwich purchased, a sandwich of equal nutritional value is donated to local charities, who, in turn, feed the hungry in the community. To date, the donations have reached more than 1.4 million sandwiches, from fourteen stores in only 2.5 years. "Eat in order to give and feed America's hungry is our call to service, and our driven mission," they say.

Life lessons they want to share with others

Michael Bart Mathews' top five quotes:

1. The best improvement starts with self-improvement.
2. If you want to make yourself a better person and make this world a better place, look into the mirror of your soul and ask yourself, "What am I doing to make that change?"
3. The moment you relinquish the power of positive thought is the exact moment that your mind is at

substantial risk of succumbing to negative, self-destructive input.

4. A personal or business-to-business relationship is not based on the length of time spent together. It is based on the foundation of integrity and trust that you build together. Build your relationships deep and strong to withstand the test of time.

5. You should, and can, accomplish many more things in life. Don't think about how it can't be accomplished; think about how you can accomplish what seems to be impossible. The word "impossible" broken down into two words spells "I'm possible," and so it should be with your vision. It's possible!

Mathews' top five tips:

1. Don't let your expenses exceed your income, or your upkeep will become your downfall!

2. You are here on earth for a specific purpose. The sooner you find your passion and make it happen, the happier your life will be, and the better you can be of service to others.

3. Don't compare yourself to others. Your everyday duty is to get off the side lines and enter the game of life. You don't have to be the first one to cross the finish line; however, you must never quit until you win.

4. If you don't know where you are going in life, how will you know when you get there? You must have a moment of clarity and develop a clear and

unwavering vision as to what it is that you want to do, and who it is that you want to become.

5. Always reach out, dream big, and believe in yourself; it's better to aim high and reach for the moon and collect several successful stars along the way, rather than aim low and hit the target of underachievement.

Mathews' top five rules

1. There is no glass ceiling, and there is no box. Your success can reach as far as infinity and beyond.

2. When preparedness and opportunity meet, the by-product brings about success.

3. It may be difficult; however, you can do it!

4. Creativity and energy flow in the direction in which you guide your thoughts and attention, whether it be good or bad, right or wrong; you have the mental power to control and direct your thoughts.

5. Success is the progressive realization of a worthwhile dream. A dream with no action is like a fish out of water trying to breathe and swim.

Why do some people experience the full effects of success, while others experience the total opposite in life? Successful people are willing to do what others don't, to live as other won't. Yes, it's true that some people are born with that silver spoon in their mouths. At birth, they received a trust fund that grew and grew and grew. Others weren't so lucky. They were born into less fortunate circumstances, which obviously were beyond their control.

Bill Gates said: "If you were born poor, it's not your mistake, but if you die poor, it's your mistake." There are countless stories of how people went from rags to riches. Like the stories of Al Pacino and 50 Cent, for example. Both were born into poverty. Today they are very successful and living a completely different lifestyle from that into which they were born.

What caused Al Pacino, 50 Cent, and countless others who were born into poverty to rise beyond their circumstances to become the men and women you see today? They were not defined by their circumstances. They understood early on that their circumstances were only temporary.

They knew in order to change some things in their lives, they had to take a realistic look, and then make those changes. You can't continue to do the same thing and expect a different outcome. That's the definition of insanity. This might sound like double talk; however, change is not change *until* you change!

Question number one: If you continue doing the same things you've been doing over the past five years, without making any changes, where will you be in the next five years? The world is rapidly changing in the blink of an eye.

Question number two: Financially speaking, if you save the exact amount of money in the next five years, equal to the amount that you saved in the past five years, how much money would you have? For some people, that's a scary question because they don't have a savings plan or can't afford to save. For others, it's a welcome thought because they can afford to save and have a regular savings plan.

Take the first step toward change by looking in the mirror and giving yourself an honest assessment of what changes you can make immediately. Now, you must simply make that change.

Author of *Financially Speaking--The Best Improvement Starts with Self Improvement--Create Your Own Economic Stimulus Plan*. **Available at** www.tmeginc.com **in soft copy and e-book formats**

ERNA BASSION

**SERIAL ENTREPRENEUR, BUSINESS COACH &
INTERNATIONAL SPEAKER**

Biography

Erna Basson is a South African woman who is rewriting the rules for entrepreneurship. With her vast experience and knowledge, she can take your business and brand to the next level. She owns multiple companies globally and has partnered with international high-profile business personalities on several projects.

WHAT LIFE LESSON DO YOU WANT TO SHARE WITH OTHERS?

You need to create the opportunities.

There will never be a point in your life where it is the right time to do a great thing. If you are waiting for that perfect moment, that perfect person, that perfect timing, then it is not going to happen. You know what you've got to do—you must create that perfect time, that perfect opportunity and the perfect situation. Your time is now!

Get out of your comfort zone.

You need to go out there and create the life you have envisioned for yourself, and the only way you can do that is to get out of your comfort zone. If you have a goal you're reaching for that takes you out of your comfort zone, you'll discover personal talent and abilities that you never knew you had.

Embrace change. How you change is how you succeed

You need to be willing to change who you are for who you want to become. Your values need to be aligned with the vision you have for yourself.

You become the sum of the people you spend time with.

You need to surround yourself with like-minded, positive people on your journey to success. Always surround yourself with people more successful than you; that way, you'll keep on growing, keep on learning, and keep on living outside your comfort zone.

Do whatever it takes

You need to be willing to do whatever it takes to achieve your goals and be successful. You must know what your "why" is. That's what pushes you when you can't push yourself. Your "why" will get you through the tough times and sleepless nights.

Erna Basson can be contacted on:
hello@erabellabeauty.com

ROBIN BOOTH

MOTIVATIONAL SPEAKER, BUSINESS COACH, PROPERTY INVESTOR, ONLINE
WORKSHOP COURSE TRAINER, ADVENTURER

Top quotes

1. If you keep doing what you have always done, you will keep getting what you always have.
2. The question is not what career I should choose, but more "What do I want to spend my time doing?"
3. Who do I need to be to create what I want?

4. *I am responsible.* There are many reasons why you think you can't do certain things. Don't let them become your excuses.

5. Those who say something cannot be done should get out of the way of those who are already doing it.

Top tips

1. When indecision is a challenge for you, understand that often indecision is the worst decision you can make.

2. Take advice from people who have done what you want to do and who are of the same profile/personality types.

3. A good place to start as an entrepreneur is asking "What lifestyle do I want?" Then do what it takes to put that in place.

4. Understand your natural flow to creating wealth, and then you won't have to work for it.

5. There is no right or wrong way to do things. There are just results. If you don't like the results you're getting, then change what you're doing.

I never believed what they told me in school about getting good grades to get a good education, which would then lead me to a good job, so I could work hard and make a good living.

And the best advice I got was realizing that we're all different, and what works for some doesn't always work for others.

Despite people calling me a successful business entrepreneur, I actually don't like business. For me, my main business is all about how I can create the life I want.

I then set up the business structures that will enable me to live that life.

So, knowing this about myself enables me to focus on the right things that get me what I want, as opposed to leading me into time-wasting ideas and activities.

As time and experiences are my currency of wealth, my income must come from activities that do not depend on my time. So, all my businesses need to be automatable and scalable.

Robin Booth can be contacted at: www.robinbooth.co.za

DAN WOODRUFF

SERIAL ENTREPRENEUR AND INTERNATIONAL SPEAKER

Biography

Dan Woodruff has a fifth-degree black belt in kickboxing, a sport he took up in 1993. He bought into a martial arts business, but after dissolving the partnership in 2004, he has been running a highly profitable business and currently runs one of the largest martial arts school in the UK. The lessons learned from developing this business have allowed Dan to set up other companies. He now spends the bulk of his time traveling internationally for speaking engagements and as a business coach to those needing help in building their own empires.

Top five business tips

Partnerships/Joint Ventures

When entering into any kind of partnership or joint venture, you must set out all terms, not just how the profit is split, but down to who does what and when. Who is responsible for all the different parts of the business (sales, marketing, staff, etc.)? When will the profits be taken, and how (shares, dividends etc.)? Who is putting in capital, and when and how will they get it back? This helps to clearly define each partner's roles and responsibilities, thus eliminating potential problems.

Marketing

Learn everything possible about marketing. The old ways are just that–old. With the Internet, things move so rapidly that it's very hard to keep up with all the changes that are happening daily. Pick one or two people you like who do internet training and follow them on social media to get their latest tips or attend their training programs.

Be consistent with your marketing. For years, I would only market when I needed new customers, and there was always a delay in attaining them, which cost me in the long run. Find out who your target market is, and where they hang out online, as in which websites they visit most, or which social networking sites they spend time on. Then, market on those sites.

Retention

You get to the top of your business by marketing, and you stay there with retention. Any business will fall apart without the growth of new customers. However, too many companies focus on this too intensively instead of looking at ways of retaining existing customers. It takes, on average, seven times more money to get a new client or customer rather than keeping one. As entrepreneurs, we need to focus on how to ensure that current customers come back to buy from us time and time again. Can you offer a discount? Offer a loyalty card system? Send them a thank you or birthday card? People buy from people, so if there's a way you can make a personal connection with your customers, there's a greater chance of them coming back to you time and time again.

Innovation

If you look at some of the top companies in their field, can you identify the one thing that has kept them there? Very often, it's innovation. Starbucks added flavors to its coffees, McDonald's always tweaks its menu, and Apple offers a new iPhone every two year. In my martial arts school, we are constantly changing the core focus of our curriculum every two months. If we taught the same kicks and punches during every class, then people would get bored and leave, so we add an extra element of training alongside the basic techniques. For two months, it could be stick fighting, then speed training, and then we change to fitness tests. By constantly teaching them new things, it gives them enough variety, so they never get bored. This innovating approach helps significantly with retaining our students.

Staff, staff, and staff

I have had one member of my staff from the beginning, and he has been outstanding. However, for years, I kept the same size business because I didn't want to employ anyone else. This was mainly because I thought no one could do anything as well as I could, and because this wasn't their business, they wouldn't care as much as I did. It wasn't until years later that I had business coaching, and I was informed that if I wanted to grow, I must outsource certain things. Your job as the owner of the business is to create and innovate new ideas and have staff to implement them. Once I grasped this concept, my company took off, and every time I delegate tasks to staff, it helps us to expand even more. Never rush into hiring staff, either–you must take your time in finding the best person, not only with the right skills and attitude for the job, but also the right temperament and energy to fit in with the rest of your team.

Bonus tip

Culture

Write out the exact culture that you want for everything about your business. Culture is the ideas, beliefs and way of life for every part of your business. You should write it out as a "Culture Statement," and have it posted up wherever people can see it. This way, you define how you want people to behave. We have an overall business culture. I have one for my staff–how they should treat one another, as well as how I shall treat them. We also have a culture for our students and what we expect from them.

Defining your culture helps give everyone clear expectations of how they are to behave and interact with others.

Five quotes I've built my business on:

Ready, Fire, Aim.

Stop sitting around, trying to make everything perfect because it never will be. Just get it started and change things as you go.

Failure defeats losers but inspires winners.

Expect to fail, but don't expect to give up. I have made tons of mistakes, but I never really see them as such because I learn from them.

The road of Someday leads to the town called Never.

You must work if you want anything. Funny enough, the harder I work, the luckier I seem to get.

When someone asks me, "What do you do?" I reply, "Whatever it takes."

There have been times when I have had to work seven days straight for months. I would work fourteen-plus hour days. But it all paid off in the end.

The more you learn, the more you earn.

The size of your library is often connected to the size of your wallet. The more you know, the more of an expert you are. And experts cost a lot of money!

Dan Woodruff can be contacted at: www.facebook.com/ Danwoodruffthekickboxer

MICHAEL JORDAN

SERIAL ENTREPRENEUR, UROLOGIST AND INTERNATIONAL SPEAKER

Biography

Michael Jordan (not the basketball player) was born in Romania. With no money, he left his hometown in 1989 to start a new life in Germany, where he qualified as a urologist. His business became the first certified EXMI medical-device teaching center of the German Continence Society in Munich, seeing between sixty to ninety patients daily, and more than 4,500 patients per year. He developed the treatment protocol for the EXMI medical device for pelvic tissue treatments, and since 2009, he's been the sole owner of this device system.

Business lessons

1. It is okay to make mistakes. I made a lot of business mistakes.
2. Read as many business books as you can and apply what you've read and learned in your business. I've read more than six hundred business books.
3. Set achievable goals.
4. Get a business coach. I have a few.
5. Acknowledge when you're stuck in your business, and don't be afraid to ask for help.
6. Surround yourself with like-minded people. You become like the people you surround yourself with. I choose people with winning and humble attitudes.
7. Network like crazy. You never know who you will meet.

Michael Jordan can be contacted on: www.facebook.com.

CHRISTINE NIELSEN

SERIAL ENTREPRENEUR, MASTER COACH AND INTERNATIONAL SPEAKER

Biography

With over 20 years of experience in transforming and driving a variety of businesses forward, Christine is a master coach and an expert at helping organizations and individuals achieve greater levels of performance and success.

What exactly does that mean? Is it necessary? If you want to get where your going, you need to let go of where you have been. People come into my office often feeling stuck, they are in some sort of transition. Feelings of uncertainty arise, and they are looking for a boost to move them to what's next. Most people go through bouts of these feelings. But not everyone seeks a coach. It is my experience that those who seek coaching are the ones that propelled themselves into achieving their dreams and goals rapidly.

Reinvention - the action or process through which something is changed so much that it appears to be entirely new. Reinventing yourself is a part of moving into the next level of performance.

To Reinvent yourself the following must occur:

1. Identify your ways of being that were once effective, but now hold you back and in fact get in your way.
2. Be willing to take yourself to ground zero. Look in the mirror and be willing to let go of the past.
3. Invent a future that is free from the past mistakes, successes and behaviors. Create your what's next. - Have a vision that is clear - Take actions that will fulfill on that vision - Take risks and don't be held back by self-limiting beliefs.

Sound's easy right? So why do so many people struggle to fulfill their dreams and goals. Why are so many people suffering and depressed in their lives, or feeling anxious and uncertain? Some people don't feel that way but that have that sense something is alluding them and they just don't know how to get where they want to go. Reinventing oneself takes work, it means being in action and looking at the behaviors that don't work in your life. Is it worth it? You tell me?

What results do you truly want for yourself and your life? If happiness and freedom are what you are up for then begin.

Begin today by taking at least one action in an area that will change your life. Complete something that has been bothering you, let go of something that is getting in your way, take that one risk that will move the needle. Life is precious. You have a finite amount of time on this planet, make the most of that time! Begin today. It's the only one you truly have.

Have Gratitude.

Exercise 9.

Name three entrepreneurs you perceive as highly successful, and why.

1 _____

_____

_____

_____

_____

2 _____

_____

_____

_____

_____

3 _____

_____

_____

_____

_____

CHAPTER 11

OVERCOMING OBSTACLES

My biggest obstacles, and how I overcame them

Personal Level

Self-Doubt and Low Self-Esteem

Because of years and years of bullying, belittling, and not able to be "in" with the other boys at school, and even in my young adult life, self-doubt, together with low self-esteem, crept in. I was very much an introvert for most of my life. I felt like I was a good-for-nothing person, and that I couldn't do anything right. I never talked to anyone about it because of the shame I felt—a result of sexual abuse at a very young age.

Later, at the age of thirty (what a waste of years!), I started going to the gym with some friends while working as a butler in Bahrain. I qualified as a spinning instructor, studied French, and all these little achievements helped me build up my confidence, step by step. I eventually took the bold step at forty to confront my dark past and went to see a therapist who specialized in sexual abuse victims. That was one of the best and bravest things I have ever done.

I attended a Mind Power™ seminar in Cape Town in 2012 and realized that I was responsible for my own happiness and success; that my mind has incredible power. I started applying the principles I learned, together with my daily positive affirmations, and I can honestly say, from that day on, my life changed dramatically, a complete turnaround! The dark demons from the past still want to come back at times, but the beauty is that I have learned to recognize and control them. They do not control me anymore.

Self-Love

For years, I battled to love myself. I could love other people, but not myself. I had a lot of anger issues and a huge temper that would flare up if someone would look at me the wrong way. I thought, *oh, well, my grandfather was like that, and some of my brothers are like that, so it must be hereditary and run in our family*. It got so bad that, one day, I decided if I didn't get help immediately, I might end up in jail. I contacted my friend, Shelton Kartun, who owns an anger management company[27] to assist me.

After a long consultation, he eventually made me stand in front of a mirror. His instruction to me: "Tell yourself that you love yourself and say it like you mean it." I tell you, it felt like hours had gone by, but for some reason, I just could not utter those words. He was extremely patient.

---

27   Shelton Kartun, Anger Management, www.angerstress.com

Eventually, with a slight whisper, I uttered the words. Then louder, and louder, and louder, until I basically screamed the words at myself. Tears started rolling down my face, and I wept uncontrollably. He put his arms around me, and I cried and cried. The weight of the world that I was carrying in the form of self-loathing and a lot of other mixed emotions rolled off my shoulders. It is a feeling that I cannot describe to anyone.

Today, I can boldly, and happily, say, without a shadow of a doubt, I truly love myself. Do you?

Hated my voice

I always had a loud voice that, most of the time, even from a very young age, would get me into trouble. My high school years were spent in the school hostel. Most of the time, I loved it. There was this one guy, two years my senior, who, for some reason, thought it was his daily duty to punish me with either his fist or a cane for having a loud voice. The result–I started to hate my voice. I would go into the field and scream as loud as I could to hurt my voice, but I just ended up with a sore throat.

When I attended Mega Sales, near Atlanta, Georgia, at Damien Elston's lake house for a five-day intensive public sales talk training workshop, we would give a presentation, with six coaches judging and critiquing us. The pressure was electrifying. To make matters worse, our speeches were recorded on a video camera. Until that time, I never told anyone I hated my voice. On day five, I had an enormous breakthrough. According to Damien, I gave the best speech, and I nailed it spot on. I received a standing ovation from the students and the coaches. I was overwhelmed, got goosebumps, and shed tears of joy. Wow, what a feeling! From that day on, I loved my voice.

Depression

Due to all the previously mentioned factors, together with financial struggles in my life, and then on top of that, the long struggle with my own sexuality, I would get depressed on many occasions. I'd go into hiding for days, not speaking to anyone. I just wanted to close my eyes and never wake up. Again, I did not speak to anyone about this. I did not want to be labeled and prescribed anti-depressants or similar medications. I struggled alone and in silence.

After a few days of feeling sorry for myself, I would start talking to myself and say, "Dude, this is not good, it doesn't do anybody any good, and you need to get yourself up and out of this state." I would then get up, go for a shower, eat, forgive myself, and finally, go on with my life.

I always talk to myself, many times aloud. I believe that talking to myself in a positive way, and reprimanding myself, has saved me many times from falling into a very deep depression. Please don't get me wrong—I'm not against anyone taking any medication for depression or other mental struggles. In fact, I encourage it because some sufferers wouldn't be able to carry on or get out of their own dark holes without medication. Depression was part of my own hang-ups.

Business Level

No financial back-up and a low cashflow

Before I developed Lubrimaxxx and Karl de L'Eau Natural Skincare in 2011, I made my living as a massage therapist. I would have little envelopes with my monthly expenses written on each one. As money came in, I would put it in the envelopes until my expenses at month-end could be paid. I couldn't ask the bank for money because I had no credibility. I didn't dare ask my parents for money because they, too, struggled to make ends meet.

When I ventured out, learning to formulate my skincare line and, eventually, my lubricant line, I followed the same principle with the envelopes. Basically, all the money I made from the treatments, apart from my daily living expenses, went into my new venture. Fortunately, I didn't have a car or other debts at that point. I bought ingredients in very small quantities via the UK, which you can imagine was very expensive due the poor Rand / Pound exchange rate. I would then make some products, sell those, and put all the money back into my business. Slowly, I started building up a cash flow. The number of massages I did to support myself and my new business ventures are legendary.

Product Credibility

Trust, whether personal or in business, is very important. Trust is earned. Consumers want to have the assurance that a new product they are investing in is, indeed, a high-quality product. You assure consumers by getting the required product credibility.

The challenge I had as a new small business owner with hardly any financial backing was to obtain the required product credibility. I was lucky because a doctor of one of my clients took it upon himself to do some research on the trustworthiness of certain available personal lubricants. Through various medical testing procedures, the results were published in an accredited medical journal. Lubrimaxxx personal lubricant was one of the healthiest and safest water-based personal lubricants for sexual activity.

Testimonials, radio interviews, and magazine articles are other great platforms for getting product exposure and credibility. One of the greatest advantages you have with product credibility is that you can sell your products at a much higher price.

Tender process–Joint Venture

One of the criteria for this huge tender that I applied for was supplying both lubrication five milliliter sachets, as well as red and black condoms. Now, I don't deal in condoms. Should I do it or let it go?

No, I love a challenge. I began asking around to find out who manufactured condoms. I eventually found a man from Johannesburg who was supplying my first client with condoms. When I approached him, he immediately agreed, and we formed a joint venture. Together, we distributed more than 19 million condoms and 19 million lube sachets to all the universities, clinics, sex workers, and safe sex campaigns all over South Africa over a two-year period.

This was where I made my first big money. Never underestimate the power of a joint venture.

Expanding (from my flat to my first warehouse)

Orders started coming in, and I eventually ran out of living and packing space in my two-bedroom flat, which was crammed with boxes and containers filled with lube. I decided to move the business to a small warehouse. With great excitement, I rented my first warehouse of 187 square meters, a little more than 2,000 square feet.

I had to hire someone with a truck because all I had was a 250cc motorcycle I had bought for cash a year before. Because I didn't have a car, I used to take those white minibus taxis for many years.

Deliveries

In the beginning, it was difficult to deliver my products. Most clients don't want to show up at your office. I looked in the yellow pages and found a guy with a small truck who was willing to help me out at a minimum rate per trip.

That helped me get back on my feet until I had enough money and credibility to buy my own bakkie, which I did. And we branded it.

Fear of public speaking

All the contributing factors of self-doubt, low self-esteem, and hating my voice led me to a fear of public speaking. I believed I wasn't good enough, so why would anyone want to listen to me? Sound familiar?

Signing up for proper public speaking training and learning how to put a presentation together, helped me to deal with my insecurities and overcome this fear. I continue practicing by myself, pretending I have a huge crowd in front of me. This is one way I prepare myself.

Don't get me wrong, whenever I step onto a stage, I still have those nervous butterflies. What I have learned is that I will always have these butterflies, but the difference is that, now, I have trained them to fly in unison.

Most fear is self-made, and in the mind, I believe. Fear can be good. It all depends on how you look at it, and how you manage it. Your reaction to internal fear determines your fate.

One definition of fear that I love is:

Fear is false evidence appearing real.

Loss of extended tender contract

The two-year contract we had for this huge tender was great, so great that I completely fell back into my comfort zone. We had the contract, manufacturing was in place, and we kept on delivering and getting paid on time. Life was good.

Then, the inevitable happened. We had to re-apply for the tender contract on completion of the original contract. We were not awarded the next tender. Oh, my word, what now? Business must go on. I had a huge warehouse, staff to pay and a lot of other business expenses.

Without a tender contract, the obvious alternative was to try to get into retail. Now, retail is a completely different ballgame from supplying nonprofit and non-government organizations. It's a long, slow process. I had no choice but to go this route. One of my strong characteristics is that I am tenacious, and I do not give up easily. Slowly, retail is gaining momentum, and more retailers are stocking our Lubrimaxxx products around the country, with good feedback from our retailers.

Low Sales-loss

Without sales, a company will have to close. Sales are the driving force for many. With low sales, it is easy to blame the economy, the state, or anybody else instead of oneself. Most of the time, we are our biggest enemy.

I started to read more and more books on sales, which boosted my confidence. I decided to outsource my public relations, and my marketing to the PR company, Get Published, which has worked on numerous high-end, high-profile clients. I was very excited to see what was achieved with an effective PR and marketing campaign in South Africa.

Outsourcing marketing and PR free me up to attend issues from my other companies.

LESSONS LEARNED

- We are sometimes our worst enemies.
- Do not be afraid to ask for help.

- Bad things happen-deal with it and get on with your life.
- Perceived obstacles are just what they are. They are there to help you grow.
- You cannot move on in life or your business unless you deal with these obstacles in a positive way and learn from your mistakes.
- Learn to LOVE yourself.
- Nobody cares about your feelings. Deal with it and grow.
- Do not be too hard on yourself. Learn to relax more and enjoy the ride. Business is a game, and not one taken too seriously.

Exercise 10.

What are the personal obstacles holding you back?

_____

_____

_____

_____

_____

What steps/strategy will you take to resolve them?

_____

_____

_____

_____

_____

Answer truthfully: Do You LOVE yourself? If no, how can you change that—now?

YES_____NO_____

Final heart-to-heart talk

There is no magic bullet or magic quick recipe for success and financial freedom. Many fundamentals have stood the test of time, and when you apply these, as laid out in this book, they will accelerate your path to success and, ultimately, financial freedom. Don't be like so many people who read a book, go to a seminar, then do nothing–eventually complaining that none of them worked for you.

Be different. Be exceptional.

NOW THAT YOU HAVE READ THIS BOOK, YOU HAVE TWO CHOICES:

1. You can either put the book down, perhaps think there was some good content, and go on with your life, or:

2. You can start by re-reading each chapter, making notes, drawing up an action plan, implementing these fundamental principles in your business and

life, and then reaping the success I've repeatedly experienced!

The choice is up to you. But, please, choose the latter option.

I have done it. And, if I could do it, what stops you from doing it even better?

Nothing, except yourself.

Your results are our success. I would love to help you achieving your success. Perhaps it will be you writing a book that shares your success story next.

ABOUT THE AUTHOR

Karel Vermeulen is a serial entrepreneur, international inspirational speaker, business and life-style transformational coach, and author. He is the owner and developer of the globally successful brand Lubrimaxxx personal lubricant, managing director of Erabella Hair Extensions, which, at the time of this publication, has successfully launched in six countries. He also is a co-owner of Communimail, Continuum Coffee Shop and co-owner of the Intelligent Millionaires Network, Cape Town, South Africa. He holds regular small accountability group sessions at his house, where he teaches other entrepreneurs and small business owners the value and importance of accountability. He knows the importance of having a business coach because he currently retains six coaches who guide and hold him accountable in reaching his objectives and goals.

He was not always an entrepreneur. Throughout his career path, he held many positions, from a police sergeant, a missionary, and working in the mining industry, to serving high-profile ministers and ambassadors as head butler for the Ritz-Carlton Hotel in Bahrain. These are just a few of the many occupations he's had. Living a healthy lifestyle is important, and he loves nature and appreciates good music and fine wine. He currently lives happily with his life partner in Cape Town, South Africa. He has a serving heart, and his greatest pleasure in life is to see other people succeed.

Through trial and error, he learned the secrets of becoming a millionaire. He made his first million at the age of forty-two, and he believes that it's never too late for anyone to make their first million. His motto is "Your Results, Our Success," which speaks volumes of his true character.

PRAISE FOR KAREL VERMEULEN

It's not often that you meet a hero. Karel Vermeulen is an award-winning entrepreneur, a best-selling author, a life-changing business and personal development coach, a highly sought-after international speaker, and yes, a hero.

Defined, that is, "a person who is admired for their courage, outstanding achievements, or noble qualities." Karel has lived a life of multiple lifetimes compared to most people, and his story is one of abuse, pain, depression, multiple failures, set-backs, and defeats. It would have been easy and understandable for him to throw in the towel on many occasions, but he did just the opposite. He created a life of perseverance, victory through defeat, and success against all odds.

Many people call themselves "coaches" or "mentors" because they have been told they are good at listening and giving good advice and making people feel good. When asked about coaching or mentoring Karel is not afraid to tell you what he thinks. "Look, I am all for making people feel better, but my focus is on telling them it's time to move forward no matter how bad you have had it or what mistakes you've made. Success is not based on your past, and it isn't determined by your current circumstance. My focus is coaching them on empowerment, more important self-empowerment."

As if this isn't impressive enough, Vermeulen isn't just a motivator, but he is a highly successful entrepreneur who owns multiple profitable companies in several different countries, and he coaches and speaks about his strategies and methods he used to create them! "I am the epitome of the overused cliché, 'If I can do it, so can you.'"

He has dedicated his life to impacting others and engaging with thousands worldwide by sharing his message without filter or apology, which is what makes what he does as an author, speaker, coach, and a hero so valuable for those who are able to hear him speak from a stage or across the table as their coach.

Compiled by Coach Dana van Hoose

www.thekvbrand.com